STORMS — OF — LIFE

LEARNING TO TRUST GOD AGAIN

STEVEN EARP

WITH JENNIFER SPINOLA

Unless otherwise indicated, all scripture quotations are from: Holy Bible, New International Version, Copyright 1973, 1984, 2011

Storms of Life
Published by ElevateFaith

International Standard Book Number: 978-0-9967377-0-8

Unless otherwise indicated, all scripture quotations are from: Holy Bible, New International Version, Copyright 1973, 1984, 2011

Published in the United States by ElevateFaith

Printed in the United States of America

For information:
ElevateFaith
10600 South Penn Ave
Suite 16 PMB 332
Oklahoma City, OK 73170

CONTENTS

DEDICATION

To the thousands of disaster relief workers who rushed to our city; to the police, fire, medical and other first responders who labored tirelessly; to the heroic educators and staff of Plaza Towers and Briarwood Elementary and Highland East Jr. High; and to the 25 precious people who lost their lives on that day:

Sydney Angle

Antonia Candelaria

Emily Conatzer

Kyle Davis

Janae Hornsby

Christopher Legg

Nicolas McCabe

Kathryn Begay

Hemant Bhonde

Richard Brown

Megan Futrell

Case Futrell

Leslie Johnson

Rick Jones

Terri Long

Jenny Neely

Cindy Plumley

Shannon Quick

Sydnee Vargyas

Karrina Vargyas

Deanna Ward

William Sass

Gina Stromski

Tewauna Robinson

Randy Smith

ACKNOWLEDGEMENTS

I'd like to especially thank my precious bride, Chrysty, for her never-ending love and support. For shining my armor daily with encouragement and then sending me out of the castle to conquer the day.

Thanks also to my kids for tolerating my long days and nights working on this. Kimmy, John-Mark, Mikayla, and Jeremy... you guys are amazing. Alyssa, my oldest daughter, helped me to spend a couple of days writing the very personal chapter on illness. Thanks Alyssa, you're a great thinker, writer, and outliner.

The staff at Elevate Church is incredible. Anthony Alan, Rhett Burnett, Rick Cadena, Candice Gabriel, Sonya Tyra, and Renee Wayland, thanks for allowing me the time to work on this project.

Thanks to Rev. James Leonard, (PhD Cambridge) for his willingness to help make sure I handled the scriptures well. I'm sure mistakes theologians find in here are the times when I didn't listen to your suggestions.

Chris Forbes, my friend, co-conspirator in mission endeavors and faith based film producer, thanks for bringing me into this project.

Thanks to the Elevate Faith team, especially Ricky Pope and Peter Friedlander for capturing on video so many of the stories in this book.

Thank You Jesus for loving me, suffering, bleeding and dying for me. Thank You for coming back from the dead three days later. Thank You for saving me.

— Pastor Steven Earp —

I'm so thankful for those of you who have stepped up to help me complete this book with Pastor Steven over the past year. It's been such a blessing—more than I can put into words—and I couldn't have done it without you.

Athos, thank you for helping me push through to the end! Obrigada por seu amor e compromisso com a nossa família. Eu te amo!

Ethan and Seth, thanks for sharing your mom, time and time again.

To those dearest of friends whose time, love, and kindness have made this project possible: Ben and Diane McCrary, Charlie and Lynn Wilkes, Don and Debra Edmonds, and the Barnes family (Dave and Molly, Hope, Anna, Lydia, and Aaron), I love you all so much!

A special thanks to Haymore Memorial Baptist Church and New Covenant for all your prayers and support. I am in your debt.

Jesus, thank You for Your sacrifice that makes life worth living.

— Jennifer Rogers Spinola —

WHY DOES GOD ALLOW TRAGEDY AND SUFFERING?

We all experience storms of life in one way or another, at one time or another.

Maybe you've experienced a loss that didn't make sense to you, such as a beloved family member who passed away too early. Maybe an illness struck you or someone close to you in a way that makes it difficult to move forward with your life. Perhaps you've encountered the ferocious winds of addiction, abuse, relational stress, disability and illness, financial storms that leave you scratching your head. Maybe you've even been in a natural disaster.

WHY WRITE THIS BOOK?

Before you read this book, I want to share with you why I wrote it. I'm passionate about the topics, "Storms of Life," and "Learning to Trust God Again." I'll also introduce you to the tornado disaster we experienced here in Moore, Oklahoma in May 2013, and how we decided to produce a feature length movie and write a book about what we learned from that incident.

I pastor a church in Moore, Oklahoma. My wife and I met here and we've lived here our entire lives. By a strange combination of circumstances, opportunities, and God-ordained moments, we have found ourselves almost continually ministering to people at the most difficult times in their lives. Our ministry has intersected so frequently with families who are suffering, that these experiences have largely defined and shaped our identity in God's kingdom. We've ministered to some who have experienced tragic losses, others who simply have unanswerable questions, and we even have extensive first-hand experience with disappointment because of an illness my wife still battles. We're continually motivated to reach out to those who are suffering.

WHY DOES PAIN AND SUFFERING EXIST?

As a teenager, I began to reflect on the question of pain and suffering. I took a hard look at the faith "handed down" by my family. I had so many questions, and there had been so much pain in life.

My critical thinking mind wondered about the philosophical dilemma. Scholars call this the "problem of pain." So many people, particularly critics of faith, have repeated the words of Epicurus in one form or another:

"Is God willing to prevent evil, but not able? Then he is
not omnipotent.
Is he able, but not willing? Then he is malevolent.
Is he both able and willing? Then whence cometh evil?
Is he neither able nor willing? Then why call him God?"[1]

The technical term for how Christian scholars attempt to answer these difficult questions is called, "theodicy."

Over time, my doubts about God and faith were satisfied. As I read the works of some of the great Christian thinkers and philosophers both from the early days of the church and also in modern times, I learned that many Christian leaders had already wrestled with these exact same questions. There are no new questions we can ask about Christianity that will cause the foundation of the faith to crumble. We just need to keep asking and seeking answers to the hard topics that commonly arise.

I still don't consider myself an expert in defending the Christian faith, but by my early 20s, I felt as if I could give a well reasoned answer to people who had questions about why God allows suffering.

My questions resurfaced, however, as suffering became more personal. It's one thing to give sterile academic answers to "prove" to others that a good God can still exist even in the middle of a suffering world. It's quite another matter to look into the eyes of a mother who has lost a child and try to offer her hope.

The first funeral I performed as an associate pastor was for a 15 year old girl just days after I had prayed for her. Before she passed away, I believed God was going to heal her. In the hospital, I looked into the eyes of her broken hearted mom and told her, "Don't give up. God can

---

1 John Hospers, *An Introduction to Philosophical Analysis*, third edition (London: Routledge, 1990), p. 310.

deliver her from this." Preaching that funeral was the hardest thing I'd done in ministry to that point. This was only the beginning of my involvement with funerals.

It didn't take long before I had performed over two hundred funerals. Some were for the elderly, some were for babies, and some were for those who committed suicide, or for various types of traumas. All of these funerals were attended by people who were hurting badly.

The question of suffering became even more personal, when my father-in-law committed suicide on Father's Day in 1998. I was changed forever. Even now, with all the healing I've experienced, I still sometimes feel regret, shame, and the desire to have a "do over" in conversations I had with him before his death.

While these previous encounters with suffering were personal enough, nothing prepared me for 2007, when my precious bride, then only 33 years old, was diagnosed with a tragic chronic illness that has impacted our family, her body, and frequently her cognitive ability. By far, this has been the greatest teacher for me when it comes to learning about what pain and disappointment does to people.

I think C. S. Lewis understood pain well when he said,

> "When I think of pain – of anxiety that gnaws like fire and loneliness that spreads out like a desert, and the heartbreaking routine of monotonous misery, or again of dull aches that blacken our whole landscape or sudden nauseating pains that knock a man's heart out at one blow, or pains that seem already intolerable and then are suddenly increased, of infuriating scorpion stinging pains that startle into maniacal movement a man who seemed half dead with his previous tortures – it 'quite o'ercrows my spirit.' If I knew any way of escape, would crawl

through sewers to find it."[2]

By the time the storm of 2013 hit our hometown of Moore, Oklahoma, I was better equipped to help people walk through a struggle. All of our previous personal encounters with suffering, as painful and devastating as they were, prepared us for the deadly storm and our ministry to people who were hurt by it.

WHEN DISASTER STRUCK OUR COMMUNITY

On May 20, 2013, the black skies brooding over Moore, Oklahoma formed, swirling into a deadly tornado that swept through the town and outlying areas without warning, flattening almost everything in its path. Wind speeds peaked at an astonishing 210 miles an hour, faster than the most modern race cars. Nearly as fast as the most aerodynamic bullet trains in Asia or Europe.

The EF5, the deadliest classification recorded by the Fujita scale, tore through stores, homes, and schools, flattening entire subdivisions killing 25 people, including 90-year-old Kathryn Begay who later passed away from related head trauma. The devastation left more than 300 people injured, scores of homes ripped from their foundations, and staggering amounts of debris and rubble where well-maintained homes and gardens had previously lain peacefully.

"It sounded like the engine of one of those big 747 planes, like it was landing on us," says teacher Sarah Tauscher.

For Gerald Bray the roar was like "twin B-52's taking off

---

2 C.S. Lewis, *The Problem of Pain* (New York: Harper One, 1940), 105.

immediately overhead, with huge thudding sounds from heavy debris hitting the roof of the school I was in," he remembers. The debris turned out to be massive rooftop air conditioning units nearly crushing the roof.

"Having been extremely close to the tornado in 1999 and the one in 2013 I can remember the strange feel in the air; it was so heavy like someone was sitting on your chest. I couldn't seem to get enough air," says Danielle Roman-Ekhoff. Danielle continued her description:

> "There was a haunting calm and silence just before the tornado roared through, and everything around shook. It sounded like we were standing in the tracks while several trains barreled past. And then there was the smell! There's nothing like the smell that I can describe, and I've never smelled anything like it. Dirt, wood, and insulation is an accurate description, but mixed with life, our day-to-day lives, the smells in each of our homes and classrooms. It's so hard to describe and even harder to relive. It's like after you see it all, you feel all the pain and heartache from each person affected. You feel all the sadness and you can't get away from the despair."

The "giant black wall of destruction," as witnesses described it in *The Daily Beast*, ripped homes off anchor bolts and threw the contents (refrigerators, mattresses, gobs of insulation) across fields[3]. The funnel cloud lofted cars as far as 100 meters away, even landing them on rooftops. School buildings and a horse training center lay in shambles. A 7-11 store caved in and killed a number of people including mom Megan Futrell and her three-month old son, Case. As the hallway walls

---

3 "Massive Tornado Hits Moore, OK" in *The Daily Beast*, May 5, 2013 (http://www.thedailybeast.comcheats/2013/05/20/massive-tornado-hits-moore-ok.html,accessed July 17, 2015).

to Plaza Towers Elementary School collapsed, seven precious children were killed.

Fallen telephone poles crisscrossed the roads like scattered straw, power lines tangled and snapped, and hundreds of thousands of construction nails littered the roadways, puncturing tires and making driving impossible. Water gushed from broken pipes, and the sickly smell of burning debris and mildew hung in the air. All around there lay broken fragments: chunks of metal carports, splinters of shattered dishes, parts of kids' toys, along with sickening tornado oddities, such as a wooden two-by-four plank driven neatly into a brick wall.

Almost as quickly as it had come, the tornado, which loomed more than a mile wide at its largest point, dissipated over a tree line, leaving unbelievable devastation and wreckage in its path.

Even now, almost two years later, many people here struggle to make sense of the staggering damage that tore our town apart. In response to the violent shaking of the tornado and the eerie "low hum-roar," as one eyewitness described the sound, many people still avoid places such as the drive-through carwash because of flashbacks.

As of this writing, construction is now completed on both elementary schools, the junior high school, and other businesses and subdivisions. But some of the scarred, empty lots that used to hold houses remain bare. The jagged broken trees, where tops and limbs were severed from the more mature bases, serve as a constant reminder of what happened.

MAKING A MOVIE ABOUT EMOTIONAL AND SPIRITUAL DISASTER RECOVERY

After the storm, we were active in recovery efforts. We gave out food and clothes. We found places for families to stay. We coordinated volunteer groups, and a host of other activities. The whole community invested every ounce of energy into recovery, then relief, then rebuilding, from morning until night day after day. Churches and organizations across our community all stepped up to help people in every way imaginable.

We heard amazing stories every day – stories of heroism and overcoming, faith and hope! It was so encouraging to look into the faces of people who had experienced a tragedy and see the light in their eyes!

Chris Forbes, a friend and film maker approached me. He said, "In a few weeks, all the media will be gone, but there will still be stories to tell. Stories of faith, hope, and overcoming, showing how God showed up even in this dark tragedy. What if we capture on video how some families recover spiritually and emotionally from the disaster?"

His idea made sense. Every day, I heard incredible stories that needed to be told. Together with Brian Cates, a local Christian short film producer, we made plans, set a budget, and started filming.

Initially, the film was going to be a local project with a microscopic budget to help people heal emotionally and spiritually. But over time, other film professionals came on board. Director Travis Palmer, then professional editor Don Stephens, and later on dozens of other artisans who helped the project to grow.

What resulted was a feature length film called, *"Where Was God? Stories of Hope after the Storm"* and also this book. At the time of writing this book, the movie has been shown in theaters in over a dozen states. It has received great reviews, it has won awards at film festivals, and it's now available on DVD in most places where DVDs are sold. These accolades are encouraging, but more encouraging are the messages we continue to receive from people who say the film has changed their lives.

Most of the stories you read here come directly from our families here in Moore, Oklahoma. I tell them as they were told directly to me, to someone on our team as we produced the film *Where Was God?* or to our video ministry ElevateFaith.com which shares stories of faith, hope and overcoming.

With so many testimonies about the storm, I've been asked a number of times if this book is about the Moore tornado.

This book is not about a tornado. The tornado was only the starting point. The stories we heard were about the *storms of life*. They were about abuse, addiction, disappointment, relationships, finances, illness, disability, grief, and loss, as well as stories about overcoming incredible obstacles. The Moore storm is the backdrop for many of these stories, but it also becomes a metaphor for any type of life storm.

Maybe you've never experienced winds strong enough to push your car off the road, but you've experienced abuse that caused you to swerve off your life plan. Maybe you've never had everything you own disappear in moments, but you've experienced disappointment that caused you to question the very purpose of life. Maybe you haven't crouched in your bathtub praying for your young kids as they cry out as hail, wind, and debris pounds your back, but you've experienced relational or financial stress that brings a similar kind of fear, panic, or even dread. I believe everyone reading this book will be able to relate to some of the circumstances and struggles we address here.

HOW CAN WE OFFER COMFORT FOR THE HURTING?

Christians sometimes offer shallow answers to hurting people. I call it "bumper sticker theology." We tell people, "God won't give you more than you can handle" or "God is going to make something great out of this."

Answers like this rarely help.

What about the philosophical answers from scholars, apologists, and professors? When darkness covers your soul, will an academic explanation give you what you desperately need? Academic answers may have their place, but rarely do they help on a personal level.

What then do we need? We need to experience God in a way that we haven't before.

I'm convinced that a life storm is precisely the time and place where you can meet the Lord in a way that changes you forever. That during the storms of life, we can more accurately hear His voice, learn from Him, and get to know Jesus.

The biggest question we've been asked is, "Where is God when life happens? When tragedy strikes? When the unspeakable occurs?"

Our ultimate goal isn't to give you the answers. Our desire instead is to give you *hope*. Most importantly, our longing is to introduce you to *Him*.

I've written from my perspective as a pastor, husband, dad, and a member of a tight-knit community that I love dearly. Jennifer Spinola is a gifted writer who has come alongside me for over a year to help capture, research, and tell stories. We've both poured our hearts and everything we are onto the pages you are about to read.

Our prayer is that as you read this book, you'll learn what we've seen in stories and principles that:

During life's storms, God is always near.

Pastor Steven Earp,
with Jennifer Spinola

1

WHEN WAVES OF DISAPPOINTMENT ROCK THE BOAT

STAY WITH THE SHIP

Before very long, a wind of hurricane force, called the Northeaster, swept down from the island. The ship was caught by the storm and could not head into the wind; so we gave way to it and were driven along.... We took such a violent battering from the storm that the next day they began to throw the cargo overboard. On the third day, they threw the ship's tackle overboard with their own hands. When neither sun nor stars appeared for many days and the storm continued raging, we finally gave up all hope of being saved.

- Acts 27:14-15,18-20 -

"It could be neuroblastoma, a common cancer for young kids. And I believe it's already to the bone."

These words forever changed the lives of my friends, Rhett and Misty Burnett. The doctor was explaining Kraleigh's test results, one of their twin girls, just five years old.

Rhett, now 53 years old, is a life-long cop. He's a big guy with a commanding presence and the personality to match. Tough, intimidating, funny, and with just enough red-neck that when you meet him, you would probably guess that he's from a small town in Oklahoma.

We've been close friends for several years now. Initially, his story about Kraleigh and how it changed him is what drew us together. I heard him tell his story at a gathering of local pastors and wanted to connect more deeply. When I see someone walk through a difficulty who still loves people, and trusts Jesus, that's someone I want in my life.

After the news from the doctor, Rhett walked down the corridor of the hospital in a daze. "I remember just kind of losing it. I was great at holding in my emotions. My granddad always told me that real men don't cry. Real men keep it together," he says. "I was really angry at God. 'How dare you do this again? First my mom, and now my child.'"

Rhett experienced the deepest kind of disappointment as he sat in that breezeway, wondering if his baby girl would make it.

Disappointment. Just fourteen simple letters describe our feelings when our experiences fall short of our expectations, our hopes, and our longings.

Rhett clearly remembers making an important decision that changed everything. He decided to look for and trust God in the storm, no matter what.

"You just start praying and believing and don't let your kids see your fear," he says. "So we started marching through that, and I carried Kraleigh into the hospital for her first treatment. And then we started to see God moving because four days later, when she left she ran out."

She ran out! In just four days, the chemotherapy treatments had actually strengthened her.

And it would be that way for two long years, watching the treatments battle the disease, sometimes winning, sometimes pulling back. And sometimes the cancer seemed to win. Their journey bounced from highs to lows: hospital visits and chemo treatments, and the loss of her beautiful brown hair. ("She's bald, but so what? So is her dad," Rhett jokes).

Kraleigh was blessed by God with a high pain threshold. "She never cried during her illness," Rhett says. "We watched her, with this incredible pain tolerance, being able to handle it, always smiling and in a good mood. I wanted to be more like that. I want to make an impact on people like she did."

Toward the end, though, Rhett began to see that God was calling Kraleigh home to Heaven.

It has been nearly eight years since Kraleigh Grace Burnett ran into the arms of Jesus, and Rhett is the first to tell people that it still hurts. Deeply.

"It was hard losing her, and it still is," he says. "She loved life and wasn't going to let anything get in her way. She had a little sticker that said, 'I may have cancer, but cancer doesn't have me.' She became this incredible hero for me to follow."

Rhett considers the two years from Kraleigh's diagnosis until her death in 2006 to be the lowest period of his life, despite the fact that he'd turned himself around spiritually in recent years. Rhett hadn't always lived the God-serving life he does now.

But a spiritual makeover didn't protect him from this life storm.

"I was confused. I made all these life and spiritual changes. I was living for the Lord," Rhett says. "Is this the way He repays me?"

The process of grief, recovery, counseling, and pain was ongoing. But Rhett clung to the Lord. He eventually felt God drawing him to get more rather than less involved in ministry. So he continued serving in his church and even pastored a country church on weekends for a while after Kraleigh's passing.

On May 20th, 2013, a giant tornado turned our community into a disaster zone. Rhett's pain came throbbing back to the surface. By that time, he was the Undersheriff of our county. As he helped coordinate first response, rescue, and then disaster relief both as a community official and as a Christian leader, his heart was broken for the parents losing sons or daughters or searching in the rubble for missing children.

"I know this ugly, brutal path that these parents are getting ready to walk down," says Rhett about the tornado's aftermath. "My deputies are going to start putting the faces of the dead children they find on their own kids. It's going to affect them. I guess God decided to use our loss for good because I can talk to these parents that have lost kids now, where I couldn't before."

The despair, disillusionment, and disappointment he saw in those days reminded him of the death of his own precious daughter just a few years before, and the crush of confusion and disappointment when God didn't heal her the way he'd hoped.

The word "disappointment" isn't quite strong enough to express what Rhett, Misty, and Kraleigh's twin sister, Calysta Joy Burnett still feel when they remember Kraleigh's forever young face. "Disappointment" is an understatement when it's used to describe much of what we'll cover in this chapter.

SOMETIMES DISAPPOINTMENT TURNS INTO DISILLUSIONMENT, AND THEN DESPAIR.

We're "disappointed" when the Red Sox don't win or the Broncos do; we're "disappointed in" our children when they gossip or get Ds in history; and we're "disappointed" when it rains on the Fourth of July parade or when McDonald's runs out of coffee.

Those kinds of disappointments are irritating for sure. But I'm talking about a deeper kind of disappointment. There are disappointments that go well beyond coffee shortages or athletic losses.

I'm talking about the devastation of a bitter divorce you never imagined could happen, and the crumbling aftermath of a life you never wanted. Or a bitter custody battle that you don't want to fight but, for the sake of the kids, you simply must. Or the diagnosis from the doctor, which in spite of fervent faith and righteous prayers, still ended in prolonged and painful death. Or the job you lost after years of commitment and sacrifice to the company, so the boss could hire an unqualified friend of his. Or the heart-wrenching, painful kind of disappointment where you've staked years of prayer, desperate soul-searching, and literally everything you have on making dreams come true, yet somehow things don't work out the way you want.

Where was He when my baby struggled for life in the NICU and breathed his last, when my father abused me for years, when my husband walked out on my children and me for another woman?

Sometimes, Christian answers to life's storms aren't encouraging. Commonly, people suffering might hear, "God gave you this trial because He knew you could handle it" or "God took your child because He needed another angel in Heaven." These platitudes, although well-meaning, can hurt like a slap in the face.

Other times, Christian answers attempt to let God off the hook by assuring us that He merely "allowed" the tragedy, and He didn't cause it. But when it comes to the condition of our hearts, saying God allowed, but didn't cause a tragedy doesn't really lessen the hurt. For in our hearts we feel that a bystander who refuses to help is equally guilty, on the same level as an armed police officer who witnesses a mugging, an assault, and stands by to watch.

THE BIBLE IS FULL OF STORMS AND GOD HAS BEEN INVOLVED IN EVERY SINGLE ONE.

When disappointment after disappointment pounds us like waves against a faltering ship, it can turn into something deeper, darker: a kind of disillusionment that gives way to despair and sometimes, even to the brink of abandoning the faith, or to use a New Testament metaphor, "to make shipwreck of your faith" (1 Tim 1:18-20).

The Apostle Paul knew exactly what it's like to be onboard a ship as the waves begin to break it apart. In the book of Acts, we get a glimpse into this dramatic story.

"When neither sun nor stars appeared for many days and the storm continued to rage," wrote the Apostle Paul as the ship he had boarded began to break apart, *"we finally gave up all hope of being saved."*

Giving up is abandonment; a slamming of the once-open door.

A Solomonic proverb testifies to the crippling power of disappointment. "While a longing fulfilled is like a vibrant tree of life, hope deferred makes the heart sick" (Proverbs 13:12).

Imagine how heart-sick Paul, the crew, and the other passengers must have been as they started throwing the cargo and tackle overboard, feverishly working to lighten the load of the ship. At the same time, they must have been sealing their hearts in a sort of painful numbness.

There is a question that surfaces in the dark hours of the night, as we are lashed by rains and the winds. I imagine while Paul was working, in moments, his heart was crying out, "God, where are You? I need You here, now, in this storm..."

But the wind continued to howl around this small, rudimentary vessel in the Adriatic Sea.

Paul, in fact, is one of the best-known biblical stand-outs for suffering and disappointment. He was beaten, stoned, and whipped badly three times. (These beatings were designed to stop just short of death – thirty-nine lashes each time.) He was shipwrecked three times, and spent one day and night in open sea. His life wasn't merely periodically dangerous, most of it was tragic.

I cannot imagine the sadness Paul experienced and the scars he carried as a result of life continually falling short of what he hoped.

In addition to the scars and physical pain Paul certainly carried on his body, he probably experienced more disappointment than we can list here. He'd been betrayed, had church members he loved fall away, had former friends try to stir up trouble for the ministry, and most of all, ached along with his churches as they either stumbled and sinned or bravely marched forward.

Paul was the former poster child for strict Judaism. In his early life, he was a brash, young student who excelled and whose energy surpassed even the greatest zealots. They'd have voted him "most likely to succeed," with his great lineage, enviable upbringing, and fanatic religious intensity.

Only now he was running for his life.

Paul, the renegade convert to Christ, was a man who knew disappointment. And he certainly knew storms.

This particular storm Paul experienced is recorded for us, in considerable detail, in Acts 27. As the chapter opens, he'd just endured some pretty nasty stuff back in the province of Caesarea, including two years of imprisonment. He had enraged a whole city by preaching the gospel of Jesus Christ. The officials eventually decided to put Paul, still a prisoner, on a ship to Rome, to let the government there decide what to do with him.

On this next leg of the trip, however, things began to change. The winds picked up, blowing them off course and their progress inched to a crawl. Sailing became difficult, and Paul warned the crew prophetically that the voyage would end in disaster.

Nobody listened to him, though, and they pressed on against the wind.

Then the storm turned ugly.

The writer of Acts, probably the Apostle Luke, records it this way:

> Before very long, a wind of hurricane force, called the Northeaster, swept down from the island. The ship was caught by the storm and could not head into the wind; so we gave way to it and were driven along. As we passed to

> the lee of a small island called Cauda, we were hardly able to make the lifeboat secure, so the men hoisted it aboard. Then they passed ropes under the ship itself to hold it together. Because they were afraid they would run aground on the sandbars of Syrtis, they lowered the sea anchor and let the ship be driven along. We took such a violent batter-ing from the storm that the next day they began to throw the cargo overboard (Acts 27:14-18).

Here we have Paul with the horror of flogging and the threat of death behind him in Caesarea, now facing disaster by sea. Hurricane-force winds were battering the ship so severely that sailors had to tie the ship together with ropes, and they dumped the cargo into the open sea in hopes of lightening the load.

HAVE YOU EVER SURVIVED A SHIPWRECK?

Dennis Hale has. During a late autumn squall in 1966 when powerful winds pounded his steel freighter on Lake Huron, the men were forced to leap into frigid waves, just a single degree above freezing. Most of the ones who leaped from the deck died in moments. [4]

Hale, a watchman who was 26 at the time, says it took eight minutes from the alarm until he ended up in the water.

"The main deck was starting to tear. You could see sparks; you could hear it ripping real slow like a piece of paper," he recalls.

4 "Shipwreck survivor Dennis Hale describes what it's like to be the only one who lived" in news.com.au, December 9, 2013 (http://www.news.com.au/lifestyle/real-life/shipwreck-survivor-dennis-hale-describes-what-its-like-to-be-the-only-one-who-lived/story-fnix-wvgh-1226778602090, accessed July 17, 2015).

> "The first thing you hear as you come through the back side is everybody gasping for air. And then the sixty-five-mile-an-hour wind hits you, and it just feels like your skin is being pulled off. By dawn, I looked at the kid in front of me, and there was some white foam coming out of his mouth. I jabbed him, and I said, 'You all right, man?' And he didn't respond."

Hale found a second man unresponsive, and when he kicked a third guy, he was alive and spoke back. They talked about Christmas and being home with family, until the man said he felt like his lungs were filling up.

He coughed and died with his arm around Hale.

When Hale was finally found by rescuers after 38 hours, he was wearing only boxer shorts, a lifejacket, and a pea coat, and he'd been floating in the life raft for more than a day, keeping his hands warm by stuffing them in his mouth. He was the only survivor.

Matt Lewis, another shipwreck survivor who floundered off the South Georgia coast in the South Atlantic en route to Antarctica in 1998, was warned at the outset of the journey to "watch for knives" in case of an emergency—that men would stab you rather than chance losing a seat on the life raft. When the fishing boat began filling unexpectedly with water, the emergency pump didn't work, and water sloshed across Lewis' feet. One life raft failed to inflate, and two guys sneaked away with the other one and were never found. Several of the guys in his raft were knocked unconscious and shoved underwater when waves slammed the raft against the sinking ship; others were battered and killed. [5]

---

5 Matt Lewis, "What it's like to survive a shipwreck" in The Telegraph, July 17 2014 (http://www.telegraph.co.uk/men/the-filter/another-mans-shoes/10970705/What-its-like-to-survive-a-shipwreck.html, accessed July 17, 2015).

About half the crew on Lewis' ship died. And Lewis was so grateful for rescue that he named his daughter after the ship that rescued him.

Not many people survive shipwrecks. And some that do, such as Hale and Lewis, aren't even sure they'd want to survive it again.

Paul, a minister of Christ who'd been beaten and stoned for the gospel, was aboard the ship, yet God still allowed the storm to happen.

With Paul in it.

He sent an angel to warn Paul about the storm, but He didn't roll back the rainclouds or still the waves. Even though He could have.

GOD COULD HAVE STOPPED THE STORM

God could have made the sea as smooth as glass at His command.

The same God who made a fish spit Jonah out on dry land and closed the mouth of lions and walked on water and raised the dead could have spared a ship, don't you think? A ship that sheltered His exhausted, bruised, and obedient servant?

Right?

The whole scenario raises troubling questions. If God could have prevented the storm, why didn't He? If He has the power to act, why doesn't He?

Acts 27:21-25 records this powerful speech from Paul to the men of the ship after the winds refused to die down:

> After they had gone a long time without food, Paul stood up before them and said: "I urge you to keep up your courage, because not one of you will be lost; only the ship will be destroyed. Last night an angel of the God to whom I belong and whom I serve stood beside me and said, 'Do not

> be afraid, Paul. You must stand trial before Caesar; and God has graciously given you the lives of all who sail with you.' So keep up your courage men, for I have faith in God that it will happen just as he told me."

It's a rousing moment for Paul—his life will be spared, his crewmates will live, and only the ship will be lost.

Except for one thing: Paul will not go free.

Maybe Paul had greater spiritual vision than most of us, but personally, it makes me wince thinking of it. Not only must Paul survive a shipwreck, but he must still go to Rome, endure further imprisonment, and then stand trial.

By this point Paul had lived in chains and under Roman guard for several years, imprisoned indefinitely in spite of the Jewish leaders offering no real charges against him, and denied a speedy trial and resolution typically offered to a Roman citizen.

Since Paul's missionary heart was constantly heavy for his churches, I'm sure he longed to be with them—exhorting, correcting, encouraging, and teaching—rather than being shuttled from trial to trial as a prisoner. And prison life in Paul's day was hardly to be envied, even for those not yet condemned. It involved dankness, filth, stench of human waste, and the perils and discomfort of being imprisoned as deep as twelve feet underground. Prisoners were manacled by varying lengths of chain and dependent on visitors (who often risked their lives to pay a visit) for clean bedding and fresh food. [6]

And yet even though God clearly had the power over life and death, over the storm and ship and sea, Paul must still remain a prisoner and plead his case at a trial among non-Jews. This surely was not the result

---

6 Bob Fraser, "Prisons in Paul's World" in *Year through the Bible* at www.mpumc.org (http://www.mpumc.org/uploads/file/Prisons%20in%20Paul.pdf, accessed July 17, 2015).

he wanted, with his freedom still out of his grasp.

Disappointment at its worst.

Certainly Paul prayed, and which of us can boast faith to equal the Apostle Paul's? We know God heard him, and cared deeply for Paul and his ministry.

But God did not grant him immediate relief.

It's a sentiment so many of us wrestle with, the answer to prayer that doesn't come as we expect it to, or as we would like it to. Or even as it seems like—to any rational observer—that it should come. And often with no palpable explanation from God.

Rhett Burnett and his wife, Misty, have painful reasons that could have caused even the stoutest of Christians to consider abandoning ship, abandoning heart, and abandoning faith.

Even though God had the power to heal Kraleigh, He didn't. At least not the way that Rhett, Misty, and Kraleigh's twin sister Calysta hoped He would.

So how, then, can we find God when the storms of disappointment come? How is it possible for us to "hang in there" when everything around us seems to be crashing in?

1. LOOK FOR HIM IN THE STORM.

As hard as it may seem when disappointment comes crashing down, especially if we're already exhausted from the fight, we can find God if we look, even if it's only a glimpse.

It's there in Paul's shipwreck story, too.

It's quick, but it's there.

He's there.

Acts 27:35 says, "After (Paul) said this, he took some bread and gave thanks to God in front of them all. Then he broke it and began to eat."

The narrative flows so quickly that it's so easy to miss, but if you back up and read it again, it's so uncanny it might give you chills. Make note of the bread, the meal, the giving of thanks.

Who else took some bread and gave thanks in the middle of a great life storm?

Who else broke bread with his friends and began to eat during the most difficult time of his life?

There's another New Testament story with some similarities. The night before His death, Jesus gathered His disciples on Passover night and shared a meal with them.

"Do this," He said, "in remembrance of me."

Do what? The breaking of bread, to represent Christ's body broken for us, drinking the wine to represent His precious blood spilled on our behalf, and the giving of thanks.

And the knowledge that three days later He would be raised from the dead, victorious.

This simple bread in Paul's hands made a powerful statement. The common made consecrated; the ordinary made, for just a quick moment, sacred simply by recognizing and thanking God for it.

A reminder of Christ's Divine presence and promises are even there in the middle of a tempest.

Remember that the storm continued to lash the boat as Paul broke bread and gave thanks; the wind continued to send walls of water crashing over the decks as they ate. The ship rocked and pitched, probably knocking men together and sending rigging scattering. Muscles ached as the seawater soaked men took just minutes to eat.

But Paul's actions echoed Christ; the One who made the seas and the clouds. The One who spoke the earth into existence. The One who slept as seawater poured into a boat on the Sea of Galilee, and had the power to still the wind and the waves with just one word.

The One who held Paul's life, and the lives of all the crew, in His powerful hands.

God, in the midst of pain, in the midst of the storm.

What about your disappointments and storms? What will it take for you to find God right in the middle of it? When desires are unmet, longings haven't been fulfilled, and dreams aren't realized, you can have great confidence that God is right in the middle of it.

Finding Him requires only looking for evidence of His presence.

While the storm rages, He is there.

And He grieves with us as we flounder through the depths of the sea-watery depths, these hard places, on the journey we never dreamed we'd have.

2. ALLOW YOURSELF TO GRIEVE.

It's common for us as Christians to hide our negative feelings, or sadness, in an unhealthy way, as if to counter any appearance of doubt or unfaithfulness. Or in some cases, we sugarcoat the trauma so it seems "better" or easier than it really is. Actually, though, when coupled with heartfelt trust in God and submission to His ways, *expressed grief opens the way to a deeper relationship with God that is authentic, true, and life-changing.*

Do you still doubt it's okay to air sadness in the face of disappointment? Look to the prophets and godly leaders of old: Jeremiah the prophet complained bitterly about his lot in life. Peter wept bitterly after realizing he had denied the Lord just as Jesus predicted - all of his brokenness stemming from the disappointment of Christ's trial. Nehemiah cried out in grief when he learned about Jerusalem's walls that were in ruins.

David the shepherd-boy-turned-king penned heartache in poetry. Joseph the young man sold into slavery in Egypt wept so loudly that the Egyptian court heard him. Hannah the childless woman wept and prayed so deeply that the priest thought she was drunk. Even Jesus wept, standing outside dead Lazarus' tomb.

Paul—the inspired author of the joy-filled book of Philippians—wrote in 1 Corinthians 1:8 that at one point he and his fellow evangelists were so discouraged that they'd given up hope of escaping with their lives. "We were under great pressure, far beyond our ability to endure, so that we despaired of life itself," he wrote.

They wept. They prayed. They raged.

Most of all, when the disappointment weighed so heavily on their souls, they grieved.

Grief is just that—a God-given, pouring out of our feelings. It's our God given response to the reality that things here on earth are not the way they should be. Grieving well is when we honor God by being honest about our full range of emotions. To tell the truth, so to speak. *And without the truth, there can be no healing.*

As the ship began to break apart in Acts 27, Paul wrote: "The terrible storm raged for many days, blotting out the sun and the stars, until at last all hope was gone" (Acts 27:20, NLT).

Did you read that correctly? The storm raged until "all hope was gone."

After working with scores of people during times of disappointment, mourning, and despair, I feel that I can say this with great confidence: *Frequently, the place of mourning is exactly where God is waiting for us.*

Healthy mourning involves pouring our hearts out to Him.

Perhaps we forget that *more than simply our obedience, God wants our heart.* All of it. He *loves* us. He loves us more deeply than we can possibly imagine, to the point of wanting to know everything we feel, on all levels, not just the feelings we've "cleaned up."

Perhaps, also, He knows that when we grieve, we come clean. We lay it all out before him. And only then are we ready to move forward, not just with the healing process, but with life.

After Kraleigh's death, Rhett eventually sought professional counseling to deal with his grief, an incredibly beneficial ministry. Emotional trauma is real and lasting. Qualified Christian counseling can go a long way to bring wounded hearts the healing they need.

"A year after Kraleigh was gone," says Rhett, "Misty came to me and said, 'You've got to go and see somebody, because you can't even talk about her.' She was right. I was afraid if I did, it would come screaming out. I didn't want to look like a crazy man, so I tried to swallow the pain."

Rhett finally went to talk to a wonderful trauma expert. This was the beginning of healing for him, but he didn't open up right away to his counselor.

"I toyed with her and danced around how tough I am," he says. "She finally told me one day, 'Tell me about the first time you saw your kids.' For whatever reason, that put me over the top. I poured myself out for an hour. At that point, I started healing."

Part of grieving might be for you to consider offering certain dreams, goals, and pursuits to the Lord, especially if they don't seem to be happening. It's saying goodbye to a dream—an intense part of our heart, our deepest longings—and acknowledging that God can bring it back "from the dead" if He so desires. If not on earth, in Heaven, where our hopes are fulfilled and realized.

Acceptance with faith—and all the scope of grief and anger that go with it—can be powerfully therapeutic and restorative, even bringing back a grieving person to life and ministry with a renewed vision of what their life might (and might not) contain.

"What you sow does not come to life unless it dies," Paul wrote to the church. "So will it be with the resurrection of the dead. The body that is sown is perishable, it is raised imperishable; it is sown in dishonor, it is raised in glory; it is sown in weakness, it is raised in power; it is sown a natural body, it is raised a spiritual body" (1 Corinthians 15:36, 42-44).

Quite simply, what we see here on earth isn't the glorious reality that we'll eventually experience. The things we see here are merely "shadows of the things to come." I like to think of this world's joys and pleasantries as a mere foreshadowing.

Like those who till the soil, we "plant" deep our aspirations, our hopes and desires, even our own physical bodies after death—with the hope of Abraham, "who reasoned that God could even raise the dead" (Hebrews 11:19).

After all, we all lose something. Miss out on something. Long for something that seems to elude us, and it still aches all these years later.

Exactly, the Bible whispers. Because you're really meant for Heaven. This world is only temporary.

The apostle wrote to the Hebrews:

> All these people were still living by faith when they died. They did not receive the things promised; they only saw them and welcomed them from a distance, admitting that they were foreigners and strangers on earth. People who say such things show that they are looking for a country

> of their own. If they had been thinking of the country they had left, they would have had opportunity to return. Instead, they were longing for a better country—a heavenly one. Therefore God is not ashamed to be called their God, for he has prepared a city for them (Hebrews 11:13-16).

A city for them, and for Kraleigh.

For Rhett, where his wife and children will finally cease their grieving and be reunited with Kraleigh, standing before the Lord face to face.

For everyone who has grieved and wondered if they would "lose all hope," but still kept the faith.

For you, who have suffered disappointments and setbacks. For you struggling to love and dream because of the fear of unfulfilled desires. For you.

Don't fear the grieving, but rather meet it with faith and honesty, knowing that God can restore, heal, and give you something new and unexpected. And He will, if you stay faithful to Him who holds you in the storm.

Listen to the aching poetry of the writer of Lamentations:

...I have been deprived of peace;
I have forgotten what prosperity is.
So I say, "My splendor is gone
and all that I had hoped from the Lord."

...Yet this I call to mind
and therefore I have hope:

Because of the Lord's great love we are not consumed,
for his compassions never fail.
They are new every morning;
great is your faithfulness.
I say to myself, "The Lord is my portion;
therefore I will wait for him."

...it is good to wait quietly
for the salvation of the Lord
Let him sit alone in silence,
for the Lord has laid it on him.
Let him bury his face in the dust—
there may yet be hope

Lamentations 3:17-29

Trust the Lord with your grief. Trust Him with your dreams. There is hope!

3. TAKE CARE OF YOURSELF.

After the storm, our lives may never be the same. Recognizing this may require an intense emotional and even physical toll on us. When we've gone through extended periods of disappointment and depression, sometimes we forget to eat properly or we don't have time. We sleep little, or not enough, or not peacefully enough to bring our souls the restoration and rest we greatly need. We pray, struggle, make phone calls, and stumble through work and life feeling like we're barely inhaling enough oxygen to breathe.

So many times caregivers or survivors of trauma face severe

burnout: a critical point where the stress is more than they can manage in their weakened state, and the body and mind simply give up.

In Acts 27:33-38 Paul instructs his fellow shipmates to do one simple thing: *Eat.*

Imagine that! He didn't encourage them to fast and pray. He told them to stop, rest, and have a meal. *Sometimes the most spiritual and productive thing you can do is take a break.*

> Just before dawn Paul urged them all to eat. "For the last fourteen days," he said, "you have been in constant suspense and have gone without food—you haven't eaten anything. Now I urge you to take some food. You need it to survive. Not one of you will lose a single hair from his head." After he said this, he took some bread and gave thanks to God in front of them all. Then he broke it and began to eat. They were all encouraged and ate some food themselves. Altogether there were 276 of us on board. When they had eaten as much as they wanted, they lightened the ship by throwing the grain into the sea (Acts 27:33-38).

Remember, *this was at the height of the storm.* Enormous waves were sloshing over the sides of the rocking ship and flooding the deck. The storm hadn't yet passed. The waves hadn't been stilled. *During the storm itself, Paul told them all to take time out and eat.* To give thanks to God. To cease a bit from the seafaring nightmare of rowing and bailing and sit down and do what they'd always done—*eat.*

It seems counterintuitive, doesn't it? Certainly the men would have had to eat to keep up their strength. But Scripture says they didn't. In fact, it had been fourteen days—a full two weeks—since they had eaten anything. Focused, day and night, hour after hour, on keeping the ship intact and staying alive.

And Paul tells them to stop. "You need [this food] to survive," he says tenderly, like a father caring for his children. Like God sending water and "fresh-baked bread" to the exhausted, discouraged prophet Elijah (1 Kings 19) when he collapsed in the desert, or opening the slave Hagar's eyes so she could "see" a well of water to refresh herself and her thirst-parched son (Genesis 21:19).

Care for yourself. Treat yourself kindly. Rest, and allow your body to recuperate from the tight coil of tension and stress. Run or walk, and get some physical exercise and sunshine. Don't apologize for it, and don't feel bad about it.

The result for Paul's crewmates when he urged them to stop and eat was that they were all "encouraged."

The sense of normalcy in the midst of chaos while caring for the physical needs of our bodies *gives us encouragement and helps us to see God.* It keeps our faith stronger so we can make it to the next round, to the next phase, to the next step in our lives.

And notice one more thing Paul's crewmates did when they had eaten as much as they wanted. They threw the grain into the sea.

When coping with difficult disappointment or stress, it's wise to let go of what you really, truly don't need. Give some of your responsibilities, if you can, to someone else. Delegate what someone else can do. Say "no" to new assignments or projects that aren't absolutely necessary, and again, don't feel bad about it. Don't only accept help, *ask for it*—and be specific.

After all, when the storm has passed and you're feeling stronger, you'll be able to pick up those responsibilities again.

Eat what you need, and then lighten your load. And see if you don't feel a wave of badly needed encouragement.

4. STAY WITH THE SHIP.

A noteworthy bit of direction in Paul's Acts 27 story comes from verse 31, right as the sailors tried to make their escape: "Unless these men *stay with the ship*, you cannot be saved."

"Staying with the ship" sounds an awful lot like faith: clinging to the once-solid footing that we may feel, in times of trauma, is about to break apart under us. Remember, when Paul spoke these prophetic words the storm was raging, the sea was foaming, and sailors were sneaking off to make a quick getaway. No one wanted to stay with the ship. Everyone wanted to abandon, to flee, to leave the wreckage behind for safer grounds. [7]

In a similar way, many people are tempted to fall away from faith, to abandon the very ship that assures their salvation. This is precisely what happens to so many people when they're faced with disappointment and calamity beyond their natural ability to bear it.

Scripture is honest about this possibility, from the parable of the seed that sprang up quickly and with joy, but "fell away" because of persecution and trouble (Matthew 13:20) to the entire book of Hebrews, which seems to have been written to new Christians having second thoughts after some stiff persecution. To those struggling with trusting Christ during difficult times, Jesus says, "Remain in me... if you do not remain in me, you are like a branch that is thrown away and withers..." (John 15:46).

Even if we've cut the lifeboats and not allowed ourselves to seek

---

7 Charles, McCall, "If You Want to Survive the Storm, You Have to Stay in the Ship," in sermoncentral.com, February 2009, (http://www.sermoncentral.com/sermons/if-you-want-to-survive-the-storm-you-have-to-stay-in-the-ship-charles-mccall-sermon-on-faith-132087.asp, accessed July 17, 2015).

unwise solutions for our pain, the struggle is still there. It's deeper. It's emotional, on an internal level, and may not even be expressed with words, but it is there. We face the temptation to distance ourselves from our faith on a small, almost imperceptible level, with the gulf widening, gaping, day after day, year after year. Platitude after dishonest platitude, until our hearts begin to forget the true, honest discourse of a believer in love with God.

When we are not honest with God about our true feelings, when we toss around nice statements rather than expressing what we really feel. It's so common for Christians to cover up our feelings. We say things like, "I'm doing okay." "Everything will work out." Or even, "God must have something better," when inside everything feels chaotic, hurting, or even angry at God. This type of dishonestly does not help us meet God. In fact, it damages us, our emotional health, the others around us; it also damages our very relationship with God.

A friend once told me, "Whatever you can't talk about controls you." We need to be able to share our deepest heart longings with someone. Definitely with the Lord, hopefully with a mature Christian friend, and many times we may need even to talk with a professional. It's important when we share our deepest hurts that we share with someone who won't pass judgment on our raw expressions.

But it's essential for us to talk out or write out our hurts and all that's involved in them.

Why? Because *our hearts are not made to deal with God in simple pithy statements*. They're meant to speak the honest and raw truth, even in our pain, and work toward a deeper understanding of His greatness and intimacy in our lives.

Even if it means questioning Him while we follow Him? Questioning God isn't the problem most of us have. Our problem also isn't whatever life storm we happen to be facing in the moment. Our problem is when we abandon an accurate view of God, His holiness, sovereignty, goodness, and work in our lives.

If we are not honest with God, or about God, the subtle abandonment begins.

Paul must have known the same truth that believers have discovered through the centuries; clinging to your faith in God's goodness and His truth during the storm is not only important, it's essential. Whether you feel it or not, please hold tight and don't let go! For that simple faith, shattered and broken as it may be, is the only thing that separates you from the raging sea and the plan God has to bring you safely to a more peaceful shore.

Without the ship, Paul and his men could not have run aground on Malta. They could not have survived the stormy sea, tossed with abandoned cargo, and they would not have made it to land, and to life.

When all else around them failed, Paul chose to stay with the ship and let it carry him through.

Rhett Burnett also decided, at a crucial point in his brokenness and shattered heart, to "stay with the ship." He remained in church, stayed close to the Savior, and let the transforming power of God begin to heal his brokenness until, at one point, he was even able to reach out to others.

Shortly after the tornado in Moore, the church I pastor was invited to host a service on the grounds of where Plaza Towers Elementary had been destroyed. Nicolas McCabe was one of seven precious kids who didn't go home to mom and dad that day. Scott and Stacey McCabe, Nic's parents, were at the service. I was honored to introduce them to Rhett.

When Rhett met Scott, he walked right up to him and shook his hand. "I said, 'I'm Rhett Burnett, and we're in the same club. I lost my daughter to cancer. Here's my card, here's my phone number. Call me in the middle of the night.' Because the middle of the night, for me, is when I struggle sometimes."

When Scott came to our church several weeks later, he still had Rhett's card in his wallet.

I'll never forget Rhett's powerful words as he told me about his connection and prayers for Scott McCabe. Two loving dads, bonding because of similar losses. Rhett said, "So my thoughts were that hopefully someday he'd reach out to me, and we could go and have coffee. If we cry like our hearts are breaking, that's fine. I'll do it with him. I told him, 'Listen, it never gets any better, but you do make friends with it.' There's a deep pain here. You wonder if it will ever go away. It never does. It doesn't get better, but it gets so you can get through the day."

Rhett was painfully honest but never lost sight of the basic tenets of his faith: That God loved him, that God loved his daughter, and that He was in control. And ultimately, that He would use even this tragedy for something far greater than Rhett or his family could see at the time.

Rhett knows he will have questions, and will always, always live with the pain of losing Kraleigh. But he's staked his faith and his future on a handful of truths: Jesus Christ, His transforming power, His grace and the fact that he can trust God with anything, even his deeply loved daughter.

And nothing can take that away from Rhett. Not life, not death, nor any disappointment in between.

Hebrews 6:19a puts it this way, "We have this hope *as an anchor for the soul*, firm and secure."

Now that's staying with the ship.

Because the storm isn't the end. God may just use the storm to get you exactly where He wants you to be, but you'll only see what God has for you if you cling to your faith, and stay with the ship.

5. REALIZE GOD IS ALWAYS AT WORK TO ACCOMPLISH SOMETHING GREATER.

My sister, Rachel Bartlett lives in Moore with her husband Todd and a houseful of kids. She believes it takes seeing *past* disappointment to see the beauty of God's plan. In her case, she never remotely imagined what God's plan was.

"When we married, we thought, 'We're going to get married, and have kids. This is the way it's going to be,'" she says. "It didn't happen. We finally decided to let God take control and steer our lives. We prayed for years, 'God, give us kids. Please give us kids.' We already had the crib and other baby items."

The baby didn't come. Year after year went by with Rachel and Todd praying for children, even trying difficult fertility treatments, but nothing changed. The crib sat there empty.

I will never forget her brokenness. Their tears. The waiting. The disappointment.

"The treatments didn't work," says Rachel. "I thought 'I am so broken. Why would my husband still want me? I can't give him what he wants, and what I want.'"

Rachel gave up. "Okay, God, you win," she recalls praying. "I'm not going to be a mom."

She specifically remembers the day she decided to stop trying and simply accept God's answer for her life, and then came the phone call from a distant relative. Something Rachel had never, ever expected.

"This lady had a baby while she was on drugs. The baby was immediately placed in foster care. They asked if we would be willing to take the baby in kinship foster care. We said yes. On Monday, the social worker called and said, 'There's a six-year-old boy, too. Will you take him?'" recalls Rachel, laughing at the memory. "And so we went from having no kids, and focusing on ourselves and our dog, to having two kids, just like that."

"Once we had kids, there was no turning back," says Todd. "I mean, we had to have kids in the house."

Since then, Rachel and Todd have been foster parents for seven years, with a total of twenty-six boys and girls coming in and out of their home so far.

Rachel, who thought she'd never be a mom, is now the "forever" mother of six—five of them officially adopted by the Bartletts. Their kitchen table is crowded with bibs and high chairs, and their house is a maze of toys, colorful stuffed animals, and little shoes. And she says a startling thing as she looks back over her life and their infertility.

"If I could go back and get pregnant, I wouldn't do it," she says. "God knew what I needed. He knew that all the pain and the sorrow and the heartbreak that we went through means I now understand a little more about the pain and the sorrow and the heartbreak that these kids who come into my home have. They need a parent who's going to say, 'I get it. We're all broken. Let me help you. Let me hold you up. Let me carry your baggage.' Just like God does for us. We're all broken. And He picks us up, holds our hand, takes that baggage, and He carries it for us."

Todd and Rachel have seen their disappointments bloom into something far greater than anything they could have imagined.

Like Rhett Burnett, their life story hasn't always played out the way they imagined.

> "It feels terribly ragged and broken to go on without Kraleigh," says Rhett. "As if a piece of our heart has been torn out with a dull rusty knife and removed, and we have been left unbandaged, and untreated, to heal on our own the best we know

how. It's a constant loss that never goes away. There isn't a day that I don't think about her. There isn't a day that I don't hurt with the same level of pain of hurt that I felt on June 4, 2006, when I lost her. The hurt doesn't stay at that level and last all day, but it is *there* every day.

"I have a picture of her and her sister that I set right in front of me at my desk at work by my computer keyboard. I do that intentionally, because I don't want a day to pass that I don't think about her, no matter the pain. It's just as raw when I think about her now, as it was then, but the more I think about her, the easier it becomes to handle and keep moving forward. Our family, though magnificently blessed, is broken, and it always will be."

But there's goodness there — purpose, and handprints of the Divine even in the storm.

Paul probably felt the same way when the ship ran aground on one of the islands of Malta, beginning a three-month-long period of unexpected adventures: surviving a deadly snakebite, healing the chief official's sick father, and after word got out, healing all the sick on the island.

In fact, Maltese tradition credits Paul with starting the first church on the island after the conversion of that same chief official, identified as "Publius" in the Bible, with a long line of bishops and churches that have survived and bloomed through the centuries.[8]

Paul went on to stand trial before Caesar as the Lord promised. But not before spreading Christianity across much of the then known world: "He proclaimed the kingdom of God and taught about the Lord Jesus Christ—with all boldness and without hindrance!" (Acts 28:37).

8 "Christianity in Malta" in vassallomalta.com (https://vassallohistory.wordpress.com/christianity-in-malta/, accessed July 17, 2015).

When disappointments come, and they will come, remember those others who experienced similar things but looked for God right in the middle of their storm. Not only did they look for Him, but they found Him, and clung to Him!

Remember Rachel and Todd Bartlett and how God revealed a much bigger plan. Remember Paul finding, trusting, and thanking God for bread as the waves crashed around him. Remember Rhett Burnett and how he ran closer to the Lord when many would run away.

Dear brother or sister, you are not alone. Keep believing.

And stay with the ship.

To hear more about Rhett Burnett's and the Bartlett's stories use the QR code below or go to www.WhereWasGod.com/book.

2

THE STORMS OF FINANCIAL HARDSHIP

LEARNING TO TRUST THE SILENCE

He said, "Go out and stand on the mountain before the LORD, for the LORD is about to pass by." Now there was a great wind, so strong that it was splitting mountains and breaking rocks in pieces before the LORD, but the LORD was not in the wind; and after the wind an earthquake, but the LORD was not in the earthquake; and after the earthquake a fire, but the

LORD was not in the fire; and after the fire a sound of sheer silence."

- 1 Kings 19:11-13[NRSV] -

Hilarey Phillips had been taking care of her ailing mom for years and raising her nine-year-old daughter, Sydnie, alone when she landed her dream job as a social worker. "That's what I was made for," says Hilarey, 43, of Oklahoma City, "taking care of people."

Helping others has always been Hilarey's specialty. I first met her in 2000. I was 25 years old and just starting to pastor a church in a poverty stricken area. Hilarey's heart for those in need has always been obvious. From starting a food pantry and clothes closet for the poor to teaching English to first generation immigrants, serving people with needs has defined her life.

Within recent years, things have started to change. Because of a bulging disc, she started having back and neck pain. Then some other strange symptoms were recently diagnosed as a type of leukemia. Hilarey started having trouble keeping up with the long overtime hours her social work position demanded.

"I was killing myself," she says. "I prayed and prayed, Lord, what do you want me to do? Do you want me to stay? Do you want me to go?"

She eventually was unable to go to work.

"I've never been in this position before. I'm paying so much for prescriptions and doctor's office co-pays that I have to juggle my bills. I started getting cut-off notices. I'd never had a cut-off notice for any kind of utility in my life," she says. "There were times when we didn't have money to buy food."

Hilarey didn't want to be "the person that was needy," she says, because she was the one who took care of everyone else.

And yet it wasn't long before Hilarey began struggling to pay for her house. Her parents and brother started keeping gas in her car, for which she cashed in her meager retirement fund to pay off, but she resisted applying for disability as long as she could. Because she was so used to helping others, turning to the government for assistance was one of the last things Hilarey wanted to do.

But she's had to make hard choices she never imagined.

"I'm literally at the point where I'm looking around my house and wondering what I can sell things for," she said recently. "I'm looking at my entertainment center, which is solid wood. Surely somebody would buy that."

And Hilarey's story is far from over. It's happening now, like it's happening to millions of people fighting recession and joblessness and low income around the world.

Many know about the struggles that accompany financial storms.

One in six Americans are on food stamps as of 2001.[9] Even the number of people with master's degrees and doctoral degrees who applied for food stamps between 2007 and 2010 has more than tripled. In 2010, five thousand people with PhDs worked as janitors, and a whopping 21% of graduates holding a bachelor's degree or higher worked as customer service representatives.[10]

And as bad as these statistics seem for some here in the Western world, even the poorest people in America seem wealthy to many who live in under-developed countries where there are no soup kitchens,

---

9 Phil Izzo, "Nearly 1 in 6 Americans Receives Food Stamps" in *The Wall Street Journal*, July 8, 2013 (http://blogs.wsj.com/economics/2013/07/08/nearly-1-in-6-americans-receive-food-stamps/, accessed July 17, 2015).

10 Stacey, Patton, "The PhD Now Comes with Food Stamps" in *The Chronicle of Higher Education*, May 6, 2012 (http://chronicle.com/article/From-Graduate-School-to/131795/, accessed July 17, 2015).

homeless shelters, or other government assistance programs that are so common in the United States.

What would you do, then, if you found yourself in the financial distress of Hilarey, seriously disabled and being solely responsible for a nine year old daughter, with no viable options?

Financial problems don't tend to just stay financial either —they can easily lead to other stressors. Relational tension is a biggie. (Can you guess the number one thing that couples fight about?) The tension can even lead to physical stress-related problems, which can be compounded if one doesn't have health insurance.

As the old saying goes, "If you got money problems, you got all kinds of problems!"

Those in financial distress are living a different life than they planned, which is sometimes a bewildering experience for Christians who've made it their goal to live a holy life: to tithe, to support mission work, and to live frugally. And still the bad financial news comes: medical bills, electric bills, insurance bills, the pink slip of dismissal.

With no warning or explanation from God. With no answer to the questions of "Why God, is this happening?" With only silence to the cries for help.

God, since you own the cattle on a thousand hills, is it too much to ask just for basic provision?

From the once confident Sunday school teacher who now battles depression as he searches the classifieds for entry level jobs, to the widow who doesn't know how she's going to pay the mortgage with her part-time library job. From the father who weeps in humiliation as he signs up for food stamps, to the family filing for bankruptcy after hospital bills overtake them.

If you don't personally relate to experiencing financial stress, then certainly you have people very close to you who have experienced it or are in the middle of it right now.

What can we do when it seems that God's response to our cries is silence?

Elijah the prophet no doubt asked this question when he fled to Mount Horeb, to the mountain of God, where Moses had seen God's glory and received the stone tablets of the law. Yet Elijah came exhausted, defeated, overcome with despair to the point of begging God to take his life.

If you're familiar with this amazing story in 1 Kings 19, you'll recall Elijah's hopelessness came after the sensational showdown against the prophets of Baal on Mount Carmel, where Elijah prayed down holy fire that consumed the altar, the wood and stones and soil, the sacrifice, and even licked up the water in the trough. Elijah and the people routed and then killed hundreds of the wicked prophets of Baal.

The curse on the drought-parched land was lifted, and Elijah ran ahead of the king's chariot in beautiful, heavenly, driving rain.

But right after that, Queen Jezebel sent a death notice to Elijah, and he fled, overwhelmed. Tired. Empty.

And more than that, questioning how God could leave things this way. How God could leave *him* this way: unprotected and unvictorious against the wrath of bloody Jezebel. Hadn't he done everything in his power to turn the nation of Israel to God? Hadn't he prayed and watched fire and rain fall from Heaven, and sensed the advent of something powerful, something holy?

Yet here he sat, shaken, starving, and entirely spent. Afraid of a ruthless queen whose hard heart had been emboldened, not won over, by the death of the prophets and the end of the drought.

Nothing holy had happened. Nothing, apparently, had changed at all!

"I have been very zealous for the Lord God Almighty," says Elijah in a voice that probably broke with despair and exhaustion. "I am the only one left, and now they are trying to kill me, too."

How common are Elijah's doubts, his confusion, and even his questioning God's fairness.

If there was a man on earth who'd "done it all," spiritually speaking, it was Elijah. He prayed. He persevered. He called down fire and performed signs and miracles. He even boldly approached the king with corrective messages from the Lord and refused to back down. This was the same Elijah God used to open and shut the heavens to rain, but now his energy and spiritual enthusiasm had run out.

And then the Lord instructed him to do this: "Go out and stand on the mountain in the presence of the Lord, for the Lord is about to pass by."

And when the wind subsided and the earthquake stilled and the fire dwindled, God had still not spoken to Elijah.

Yet.

Until Elijah heard the "gentle whisper," (1 Kings 19:12, NIV) and he covered his face and came to the mouth of the cave.

There is nothing in the text to indicate that the "gentle whisper" or "sound of a gentle blowing" (NASB), or "still, small voice" (KJV) was God's voice, but Elijah seemed to recognize immediately that it was. Interestingly enough, this "gentle whisper" in the NIV is translated in the New Revised Standard Version not as a verbalized "noise" at all, but as *"a sound of sheer silence."*

When Elijah desperately needed answers, God gave him silence.

There was no explanation for Jezebel's vicious threats even in the face of her false prophets' clear defeat. There was no answer for what lay ahead for Israel's future, and why the restoration of its people seemed so long in coming. There was no apology for the exhaustion, the running, the hiding in caves, and the maddening game of hide-and-seek with King Ahab.

And there was no verbalized thanks either, for Elijah facing down the prophets of Baal, or convincing the people of Israel that God was really God.

Just silence when it came to the answers Elijah desperately wanted.

Have you ever cried out to the Lord and received nothing but what seems to be silence? The bills get turned over to a collection agency, the car breaks down with no money for repairs, and the bill from the specialist is double what you expected.

Hilarey Phillips is there now, after all her years of service to the poor and to the Lord.

How can we respond when we weep, pray, beg God for support and still remain faithful while our resources are depleted, and God is silent?

Elijah was not the only one who faltered in the face of unanswered questions. His heart cry echoes the questions we ask when we find ourselves in a difficult circumstance and no answer is in sight.

God asked Elijah the same question twice: "What are you doing here, Elijah?"

Instead of God giving the answers Elijah longed for, God Himself gave short responses and asked questions of His own.

Probably the only thing worse than getting short answers from God is getting no answer at all. Did God not have an answer for the most faithful of His servants? Is He really so heartless that He would refuse to answer, dodge the issue, change the subject?

In Elijah's case, the silence was eventually broken. Elijah's course was reset as God instructed him to pass along his ministry to Elisha and then Elijah was taken up into Heaven in a whirlwind.

John the Baptist is another example of a believer experiencing temporary, painful silence. When John was imprisoned for preaching the gospel of the Kingdom of God, he sent a simple question to Jesus, "Are you the one to come, or should we expect someone else?" (Matthew 11:3) Jesus sent word about the miracles that surrounded His ministry, but shortly after that, John was beheaded. This was surely not the answer John longed for.

In the case of Job, God was silent for 36 chapters of torturous misery. Job wanted to know why he had lost everything. So he cried, wept, screamed and fumed. He even demanded an audience with God. When God finally spoke to Job, He still didn't give a response to Job's pain. God did not give the answers Job so desperately wanted.

So why this mysterious absence of answers? After the roar of fire and shaking rocks and wind, of layoffs and insurance premiums and late fees, we hear nothing but stillness. A whisper, a breath, the faintest of sounds that still does not give a response to our pain, and our financial dilemma.

Dear Lord, please give me anything but this stifling stillness...

While we cannot know the mind of God, or answer the questions that only He can address, we can find several principles from Scripture that address His sometimes unnerving silence.

What are some principles that can help as we long to hear His voice while in the midst of financial turmoil? When it seems the only answer we get from God is silence?

1. SOMETIMES GOD WANTS ME TO USE THE WISDOM HE HAS ALREADY GIVEN ME.

Not all financial problems are the same. Some are self-inflicted, while others are thrust upon us due to no fault of our own. We'll first take a look at what we can do to ensure that we are not personally causing the financial struggle we find ourselves in.

Sometimes, the reason God seems silent on something is because He's already given us the exact answers and tools to get ourselves out of the fix we find ourselves in. Why would He speak to our hearts if He has already communicated something to us plainly and we aren't acting on it? Is this you? If you want to find out, then keep on reading.

Talking about finances is a complex issue for me as a pastor. Americans seem to be more private about what they do with their money than what they do in the bedroom.

How can I communicate about finances in a way that meets the needs of everyone? Can I give comfort to the hurting, and challenge the able bodied who need to take more initiative, and also encourage the wealthy to empathize with those in need?

The American Christian view of money tends to be a study in extremes.

On the one hand, some suggest its God's plan for everyone to be exceedingly wealthy, and if we follow His plan and have enough "faith," then our wildest dreams will come true.

In 2001, I was operating a party planning company when our office manager contacted me. He wanted to talk about a bounced check written to us. We received insufficient checks on a semi-regular basis. So I wondered why I needed to meet with him about this particular check.

Imagine my surprise when I saw the check had come from a local church!

"Of course, this must be a mistake. It's probably a bank error," I thought to myself. "I'll call the pastor to straighten it out."

My conversation with the pastor was one of the most bizarre I can remember. His response to the bounced check he had written: "Well, I knew we didn't have the money to pay for the event, but we have faith. I just write the checks and trust God to fill the bank account to cover it."

Yes. Really.

This church was an example of prosperity and faith theology taken to a degree of absurdity.

We also see examples from the other extreme. Some eschew material wealth under any circumstances. When they read in the King James Version that "the love of money is the root of all evil" in I Timothy 6:10, they take it to mean that everyone should take a vow of poverty and give everything away similar to the life famously lived by Mother Theresa.

I have great respect for those who literally give everything away for the sake of the gospel and for those less fortunate. But does the Lord require such from us? More than that, is it okay for us to pass judgment on families who happen to be well resourced?

Does the Bible give us a clear path that sorts these issues out? How are we to deal with matters of wealth, poverty, finances, and prosperity?

We get a clear answer from Matthew chapter 25.

Check out verses 14-15: "Again, it will be like a man going on a journey, who called his servants and entrusted his wealth to them. To one he gave five bags of gold, to another two bags, and to another one bag, each according to his ability. Then he went on his journey."

In the story of this landowner who entrusted his wealth to several servants, the application is plain. God is the Master and He owns it all. We're just His managers taking care of things for Him during this short lifetime we'll live here. The common biblical term for this is "stewardship."

So, how does the Master expect us to take care of the resources He has loaned to us? Did He leave us any instructions? You bet He did. Loads of instructions. In fact, Evangelist Greg Laurie says this, "It is worth noting that money is such an important topic in the Bible that it is the main subject of nearly half of the parables Jesus told. In addition, one in every seven verses in the New Testament deals with this topic. The Bible offers 500 verses on prayer, fewer than 500 verses on faith, and more than 2,000 verses on money." [11]

Why so much emphasis on money? Laurie addresses that too. "There is a fundamental connection between our spiritual lives and how we think about and handle money."

What's the content of all these verses on money? In many instances, God has already given us prescriptive instructions that when followed, financial ruin will be avoided or at least lessened.

The main way God addresses finances is through wisdom. The book of Proverbs in large part is devoted to brief catchy truisms. The principles found there and many other places in the Bible can help us get a handle on how to best manage what He has entrusted to us.

Here are a few samples of what we can learn from Scripture about

---

11 "Money and Motives" Greg Laurie, *A New Beginning*, no date (http://www.oneplace.com/ministries/a-new-beginning/read/articles/money-and-motives-9220.html, accessed July 18, 2015).

money (there are hundreds more!):

- » Don't serve money. | Matthew 6:24
- » Don't spend your life seeking wealth that disappears. | Proverbs 23:4-5
- » Don't trust in money. | 1 Timothy 6:17
- » Track your finances. | Proverbs 27:23-24
- » Plan your spending. | Proverbs 21:5
- » Save for the future. | Proverbs 21:20
- » Give 10% back to Him. | Malachi 3:10
- » Enjoy what you have. | Ecclesiastes 6:9
- » Work hard. | Colossians 3:23
- » Be industrious. | Proverbs 10:4

Many people are surprised the Bible addresses all these things. But this list is just the beginning. We can also learn about borrowing, co-signing, investing, and more.

Financial Peace University by Dave Ramsey and Crown Financial are two great Christian programs. You can find them both online to get a thorough understanding and practice of some solid principles. Many people have experienced financial freedom by simply learning basic financial principals and following through to make them work.

In fact, Hilarey Phillips believes that deciding to tithe, even with medical bills up to her ears, ushered in an unprecedented time of financial gifts for her.

"I heard God saying, 'I want you to tithe.' And that was in the middle of all of the medical bills," she recalls. "But then all of these [gifts] came rolling in!"

Why would I address God's principles for handling money in a book on "finding God in life's storms?"

After 22 years of ministry, I have found that most folks do not understand what God has already said about finances. Many financial storms can be self-corrected simply by being better educated and disciplined. So if you've ever said, "I just don't know where it all goes..." then please check out Financial Peace or Crown Ministries.

But not every financial problem is self-inflicted.

Elijah's story isn't specifically about finances, but it *is* about provision, desperation, and longing to hear from God. In the life of Elijah, he was right in the center of God's will, being obedient, faithful, and disciplined even at the risk of his own life. Even in Hilarey's story, we see a set of circumstances well beyond her ability to control.

Sometimes God's silences are because He's already spoken to us about the issue in His Word. But what about the times God is silent and our problems could not be avoided? When we've done all we know to do? When we've taken every step possible?

2. SOMETIMES SILENCE MEANS GOD WANTS TO SHOW US SOMETHING GREATER.

There is another instance of divine silence—and what appears to be purposeful delay—in John 11. When word came to Jesus that His friend Lazarus was sick, He didn't hurry there immediately. Instead, He stayed where He was for two more days. And in the meantime, Lazarus died.

"Lord," Martha said to Jesus in verse 21, "If you had been here, my brother would not have died."

Mary echoed the same words later in verse 32—and I can't help but sense despair, perhaps even a twinge of bitterness, because of Jesus' apparent disregard. After all, they'd sent word to Him, no doubt as quickly as they could. And still He lingered. He didn't come. He didn't answer.

In this case, Jesus wanted to show them something greater than simply healing Lazarus from his sickness. Jesus wanted to raise him from the dead. Jesus' delay was calculated, and motivated by unsurpassed love and joy, to bring Mary and Martha a greater blessing than they would have received otherwise.

For some reason, Jesus in his wisdom, allowed Mary and Martha to remain uninformed about His intentions – the intentions for a glorious miracle of watching Lazarus walk from the tomb, four days dead and still wrapped in grave clothes.

A man healed from sickness is one thing, but a dead man raised to life? That's quite another story. That's the gift Jesus wanted to give Mary and Martha.

Whatever your situation, there's a gift He wants to give you, too.

For starters, God wants to give you Himself. In every hardship or trying situation, keep in mind that you are being privileged with a new revelation of who God is *in an extremely personal way.* There are no cosmic accidents. No mix-ups with the script. As hard and unfair as it may seem from human eyes, Scripture assures us that every trial, including this specific financial crisis you're in, came to you from the loving hand of your heavenly Father. For *you*.

And not solely for the purpose of "teaching" you something, either. Not always. Sure, He's always bringing us to a deeper and higher level, and teaching is part of that. But far more than "teaching" and "lessons," God cares about the heart. *Your* heart. He cares about *you*.

He wants to give you Himself.

In Hilary's case, God encouraged her by building her daughter Sydnie's faith as she watched Him provide through the hard times. A bag of groceries here, a tank of gas there, and an unexpected check there. "Wow, Mom, God is really helping us," said Sydnie, as her own young and shining faith blooms.

He's encouraged Hilarey, too. "I never thought I'd be in this situation. But I know somehow, no matter what, God is going to provide."

And He has provided, from random gifts of money to anonymously paid utility bills. Trusting in the grace and faithfulness of God, Hilarey has found the strength to push through—even with her often excruciating physical pain—to the next part of God's plan for her life. A life which now includes community, and leaning on others for help.

"You don't know what you are capable of until you are pushed and you have no other options," she says. "The eight years I spent trying to go above and beyond with helping people? He's turned that all back around. He said, 'All your life you've tried to put up the wall and keep people out, and you've taken care of everyone else but yourself, but you can't do this on your own.'"

That's one of the ways God has drawn near to Hilarey. Not answering her questions or supernaturally healing her—yet—but providing for her family's needs in His silent, secret ways.

In each and every crisis, we can learn things about God that

we've never before known. To Moses, the refugee in the desert, He appeared in a burning bush. And it's the only case of a burning bush anywhere else in the entire Bible. To Job, He spoke from a whirlwind. To Shadrach, Meshach, and Abednego, He walked in the fiery furnace. To Paul, He thundered from the sky.

And to Elijah, He sent a soft blowing, a gentle breath, or a still silence. We don't have any record of these incidents being repeated. Such specific, personal manifestations of God's presence were intended to convey something to these particular people, in these particular ways.

What gift has God sent you? What is He showing you of himself? Of His character? Of His relationship to you, and only you, in a way you alone understand? Like Mary and Martha grieving over Lazarus, remember that so often God waits to bring a greater revelation; a greater knowledge of Himself; a greater gift.

If He hasn't made it clear to you yet, don't rush the process—wait, pray, and ask Him to open your eyes to this new side of Him He's preparing to reveal. Are you willing to walk through it with Him, like lovers walk through sickness and pain together, never abandoning one another even in the throes of tragedy?

Wait, then, for His answer, His gift, because it will come. Perhaps this greater understanding of God will come for you soon, or now, in this life. But if not, the day will come when you see Jesus face to face and every curiosity and longing will be fulfilled.

And it will be greater than anything He could have given you if He had answered your prayer exactly the way you had wanted.

3. THE SILENCE MAY JUST BE GOD GRIEVING WITH US.

In the Old Testament book of Job, we find another suffering and suddenly impoverished man who loved God. Perhaps we can gain some more insight for understanding God's silence in this book, and especially from Job's infamous buddies.

Now, the false friends of Job have gotten a pretty bad rap over the years for their smug accusations, and their insistence that poor Job must have done *something* wrong to deserve all this. We know from a peek at the story that Job was innocent. It's easy to point the finger at these guys for their horrible advice, but initially, they did everything right.

At the beginning of the book, after Satan inflicted Job with sores, the death of his children, and extreme financial loss leading to utter ruin, we see these friends doing something extraordinary and beautiful:

> When Job's three friends, Eliphaz the Temanite, Bildad the Shuhite and Zophar the Naamathite, heard about all the troubles that had come upon him, they set out from their homes and met together by agreement to go and sympathize with him and comfort him. When they saw him from a distance, they could hardly recognize him; they began to weep aloud, and they tore their robes and sprinkled dust on their heads. ***Then they sat on the ground with him for seven days and seven nights. No one said a word to him, because they saw how great his suffering was***" (Job 2:11-13).

The text says Job's suffering was so "great" that "no one said a word" to Job. The silence of grief, of love, of deepest compassion, and sympathy. Not cold-heartedness, but pity. Not aloof detachment, but personal devastation. They wept out loud, they tore their robes, they sprinkled dust on their heads, and they sat together in silence for *an entire week.*

In scripture, we read much about how God empathizes and comforts us (2 Corinthians 1:3-5; Romans 8:26; Hebrews 4:15 and others). Jesus wept tears of compassion over Jerusalem (Luke 19:41). He mourned with the family after Lazarus died (John 11:35). Since we're called to "mourn with those who mourn" (Romans 12:15) it seems reasonable that at times, God's silence may indicate that He is in fact, grieving *with* us and drawing close to us in ways that we never could have experienced otherwise.

Is it possible that when God looked on Elijah's suffering heart—his exhausted spirit, his dejection—that He simply remained silent out of love and compassion? The intimate, wordless sympathy that is even too great for tears?

So often when we don't hear from God, the first thing many Christians imagine is His angry, cold, brooding silence His turned head, the "closed" sign on His door. We assume that God operates on the same level we humans do, treating us with spite or vindictiveness, or putting up stony walls. He's given us the silent treatment again, and now we have to scramble to find out why, or what we've done *this* time.

But this is God we're talking about. Not a thin-skinned, tangential deity who hurls lightning bolts and storms off in a pouting huff at our every infraction. This is our God: "slow to anger, abounding in mercy," whose "kindness leads us to repentance."

What we see from the story is that God wasn't angry at Elijah at all, or even distant. In fact, what seemed like inaction on God's part was not, but instead, *God came close to him in quiet sorrow.* The faint breath, the still small voice outside the cave was not condemnation. It was possibly loving empathy.

What if God the Father, in His deep compassion, drew near to His servant Elijah in a tender, personal way and simply sat by his side, a fellow partner in suffering and grief? If anyone saw what the bold, faithful warrior prophet had suffered through, God did. He knew. And He would, one day, make it right.

We know from previous verses that God cared for Elijah's deepest needs like a father holding a son He loves. When Elijah collapsed on the journey to Mount Horeb, shattered and drained of spiritual and physical energy, God sent an "angel of the Lord" to furnish him with fresh-baked bread and water to drink. Twice the angel gently woke Elijah from sleep, encouraging him to eat, "for the journey is too much for you" (I Kings 19:7).

Could God be simply drawing near to us in divine sympathy— the stuff of friends, the intimate language of those who are close, weeping as we walk through the dark times together?

You might describe it as "deep calling to deep," a reference to Psalm 42:1-5, where the psalmist cries out to God in these poignant words:

As the deer pants for streams of water,
so my soul pants for you, my God.
My soul thirsts for God, for the living God...
My tears have been my food
day and night,
while people say to me all day long,
"Where is your God?"...
Why, my soul, are you downcast?
Why so disturbed within me?
Put your hope in God,
for I will yet praise him,
my Savior and my God...

Deep calls to deep
in the roar of your waterfalls;

all your waves and breakers
have swept over me.

The force of sheer emotion here is too strong for words, leaving space for only the silent communion of soul and spirit with the heart of God and the sounds of nature's waterfall.

James White, a North Carolina pastor, tells of a time when his four good friends were killed in a car crash, and he was supposed to have been with them. A young college student not yet committed to Christ, White was blindsided by the news. To sort it all out, he took a walk to the empty college football stadium and sat in the moonlight, reflecting on the loss of his friends, and how close he had come to dying with them.

"I remember crying out to God to help me sort it all out, to make sense of it all," writes White. "To talk to me...to say something ... anything! Silence. In truth, it was one of the deepest conversations we had ever had. He was speaking to me, moving within me, communing and communicating with me on levels that had never been opened to Him before. It was the start of many conversations, some even more traumatic. Within four months I became a Christian."[12]

White goes on to write that it is extremely important for Christians to consider it's not dead silence that we hear when God doesn't appear to be speaking. Rather, he says, it's a "pregnant pause; a prompting to engage in personal reflection so that the deepest of answers, the most profound of responses, can be given and heard. This is the mark of all master-teachers."

C.S. Lewis, Christian apologist and writer, records his intense

---

12 "The Silence of God," James Emory White, in *Church and Culture*, Sept 26, 2013 (http://www.churchandculture.org/Blog.asp?ID=4917, accessed July 18, 2015).

sorrow over the death of his beloved wife, Joy, after her slow deterioration from cancer. And when he needed it most, he felt a void when he tried to pray, tried to hear from God, tried to make sense of the pain.

"Where is God?" Lewis wrote in his book *A Grief Observed*.[13]

> "When you are happy, so happy that you have no sense of needing Him... But go to Him when your need is desperate, when all other help is vain, and what do you find? A door slammed in your face, and a sound of bolting and double bolting on the inside. After that, silence. You may as well turn away. The longer you wait, the more emphatic the silence will become... Why is He so present a commander in our time of prosperity and so very absent a help in time of trouble?"

Lewis' grief after Joy's death seems desperate. Yet after long years of healing for Lewis, he describes his grief in more hopeful language. He wrote, "I have gradually been coming to feel that the door is no longer shut and bolted ... [I was like] the drowning man who can't be helped because he clutches and grabs."

Clutching and grabbing describes all of us at one time or another, frantically searching for answers, for relief, for something to make it all right again. Assuming the worst of God, and in multiplied anguish, turning away. But in fact, God may be giving us one of the greatest blessings we've had yet: His solace and pity, and His grief as one dear friend for another. Words too deep for speech, and love too pained for conversation.

He will speak in time. He always does. Listen first for the silence,

---

13 C. S. Lewis, *The Complete C.S. Lewis Signature Classics* (New York: HarperOne, 2002), 658.

for the gentle breath of God's quiet in your life. Cease your striving, and rest in Him. *Rest in Him!*

And soon enough, He will speak.

4. GOD ALWAYS PROVIDES FOR OUR GREATEST NEEDS.

If you've been a Christ follower for any length of time, you've heard sermons and stories about God's provision. You know about how God sent manna for the people of Israel in the wilderness and how Jesus multiplied loaves of bread and fish to feed more than five thousand hungry people. How He routed besieging armies so that the starving villagers could plunder the camps and eat their fill.

But when we're waiting like Hilarey for enough money to pay the electric bill (before it gets cut off), and we just spent the last few dollars of our paycheck on rent and groceries, the wait sometimes seems interminable. Even unfair.

And while we know God provides, we sometimes assume He's going to do it in one of the neater, more orthodox ways He did in Scripture. A multiplied lunch? Sure. Oil and flour that never run out? Great.

But sometimes God chooses less conventional ways to provide for His people in need.

Like... ravens.

Yep. Birds. And we're not talking pretty white doves, either. Ravens are scavengers.[14]

---

14 See Ray Pritchard's sermon transcript, "Elijah and the Ravens," Mar 7, 2006, at keepbeliving.com (http://www.keepbelieving.com/sermon/elijah-and-the-ravens/, accessed July 18, 2015).

Take Elijah again, several chapters before his weary flight to the mountains, when Israel lay parched under severe drought, which came as one of God's judgments for the country's wickedness. Note that Elijah, a righteous man, did not commit the gross sins Israel was being punished for—the idolatry and rebellion against God. Elijah was a prophet of Almighty God, a speaker of truth and judgment, and a worker of signs and miracles in His name. He had given his life to the Lord irrevocably, with power and faithfulness.

Yet God did not spare Elijah from the same affliction that the rest of the country endured: drought and famine.

I Kings 17:2-5 explains:

> Then the word of the Lord came to Elijah: "Leave here, turn eastward and hide in the Kerith Ravine, east of the Jordan. You will drink from the brook, and I have directed the ravens to supply you with food there."
>
> So he did what the Lord had told him. He went to the Kerith Ravine, east of the Jordan, and stayed there. The ravens brought him bread and meat in the morning and bread and meat in the evening, and he drank from the brook.

And so Elijah survived the drought for a season by receiving food delivered to him by scavenging birds that were deemed "unclean" and detestable to the Jewish people.

This story is interesting for reasons in itself, but we can also glean some principles to help us through financial hardships.

For starters, the drought in Israel lasted three and a half years (James 5:17). If Elijah stayed at Cherith the entire time, the ravens brought him more than two thousand meals. *Two thousand meals!* All brought at the command of God, without costing Elijah a penny. Elijah never even had to ask for it.

"It would take some detailed calculations to figure out how much we've spent on food over the years, but God knows the exact amount because he keeps track of what we need," writes Ray Pritchard, a Texas pastor and ministry leader. "He knows your name and he knows your address and he knows what you need today and he knows what you will need tomorrow. *It's all written on his heart because he watches over you even when you think he has forgotten you.*" [15]

It's fascinating to me how God creatively provides for us at times.

Meet Peter Friedlander, a volunteer who helped with tornado relief in Moore and can vouch for God's provision during a time of thin financial resources. Peter spent two semesters in Israel studying Christian media and subsequently doing media work for a Palestinian Christian mission organization in Bethlehem, even traveling throughout Israel documenting on video the stories of Christ followers there.

Peter went home for Christmas with all kinds of job references, expecting to land a solid job or ministry role quickly, but none of the contacts panned out.

While Peter was still searching for a job, the 2013 tornado wrecked the city of Moore. Peter felt a strong compulsion to come here and help out.

A month after the storm, Peter headed to Moore with only his car and about $500 cash—nothing else. His only connection to the local community was a non-profit he found on the internet that was established by churches in Moore to help coordinate disaster relief efforts. Still he kept going, determined to honor God during his period

---

15 "Elijah and the Ravens," Mar 7, 2006, at keepbeliving.com (http://www.keepbelieving.com/sermon/elijah-and-the-ravens/, accessed July 18, 2015).

of joblessness.

"By the time I got to Oklahoma I didn't have much left in my checking account, but I continued to help wherever I could in Moore," he says. "And it seemed like whenever my gas tank was less than a quarter full somebody would randomly walk up to me and hand me some cash or a gift card for groceries."

When he had only about two more weeks of money left, Peter began to earnestly look for work in the Moore area, and what caught his attention most was what people were saying.

Hearing story after story, God allowed him to cross paths with our church, Elevate Church, in Moore, Oklahoma. We were also hearing and documenting stories of hope, faith, and overcoming. His connection was perfect timing for us. We needed someone to help us record stories of life change, and Peter wanted to use his gifts and abilities for furthering God's Kingdom. Peter helped us launch the website ElevateFaith.com where we continue to share stories of faith.

Peter walked right into his job simply by doing what God had put in his heart.

Just like He did for Peter Friedlander, and for Elijah, God will send help at the proper time, even if His ways of provision are anything but orthodox. God not only uses unusual methods in providing for His people, but at times He seems to specialize in it!

Of course we'd prefer that God fill our pockets to abundance and our purses to overflowing, but sometimes He prefers to work in more interesting ways, even working within our times of lack.

In the Western world, it's common for Christians to consider wealth as the only way God blesses us. But as great as wealth is, it is still temporal, passing, and should be treated as such. Neither wealth nor poverty are a sign of spirituality. In scripture, we see godly and ungodly people alike in both extreme poverty and extreme wealth.

So is wealth a gift from God? Most assuredly so. Just as the air we breathe and the sun we enjoy.

What might be more surprising is that poverty also can be a divine gift.

Consider James 1:9-10 : "Believers in humble circumstances ought to take pride in their high position. But the rich should take pride in their humiliation, since they will pass away like a wild flower."

Did you catch that? The startling paradox of God? The inversion of worldly versus Divine value? *James called riches a "humiliation," but "humble circumstances" a high position!*

It's a high position because it gives us the gift of waiting on God like Elijah did, and seeing Him provide for us, day by day, in ways we've never imagined. It is those who have suffered through the droughts, through the dry seasons, through the days of financial hardship that have learned to wait on Him most, to lean on Him most. To know Him in ways that others might not be able to grasp.

A gift, indeed.

A strange gift in the eyes of the world, like bread and meat from ravens. But a Divine gift nevertheless.

When the brook dried up (1 Kings 17:7) God had another means of provision waiting for Elijah: a widow in Zarephath was in desperate need. Elijah's stay at this widow's home contributed to two incredible miracles. One time oil and flour were supernaturally replenished to feed them all. In another spectacular show of power and faith, Elijah was used by God to raise the widow's son from the dead.

In like manner, centuries later, Jesus demonstrates that He is the resurrection and the life. He takes the hand of a dead girl and raises her gently back to life. He goes to the tomb of the dead man Lazarus and calls, "Come out!" And again, at Nain, He stops a funeral procession and makes the burial of a widow's son unnecessary.

More than all these, Jesus, the God-man, the Son of God, was cold in the tomb for three days until God raised Him from the dead forever. This proved that Jesus is the great Provider, who overcame death and the grave and promises to meet all of our needs.

Trust Him to meet your needs. All of them, in His way, and in His time. For He is more than able to do it.

He provided for Elijah, for Peter Friedlander, and for Hilarey Phillips. And He can do it for you.

This brings me to my final thought on the subject.

5. WE GENERALLY HAVE MORE ALREADY THAN WE THINK WE DO.

Back in 1 Kings 19, Elijah's main complaint—which he voiced twice, word for word—was that he'd been left alone to do God's work.

"I have been very zealous for the Lord God Almighty," Elijah said in verse 14. "The Israelites have rejected your covenant, torn down your altars, and put your prophets to death with the sword. I am the only one left, and now they are trying to kill me too."

While Elijah's complaint and exhausted despair was perfectly understandable, God gave Elijah an interesting response. First, God told him to go back the way he'd come and anoint Elisha as his successor.

And then He addresses Elijah's grievance about being the only one left: "Yet I reserve seven thousand in Israel all whose knees have not bowed down to Baal and whose mouths have not kissed him."

Wait a minute—seven thousand? Elijah thought he was the *only one* left, and God had set aside *seven thousand* believing Israelites who had kept the faith and rejected the wicked religion of Baal worship.

Perhaps if Elijah had known this, might he have avoided such deep discouragement?

Regardless, Elijah had more than he thought he did all along. He wasn't alone. He just failed to realize what God had already done in his life, and for the growth and glory of Israel.

And I would suggest that the same might be true of us. When we think we're in dire straits, could we possibly be overlooking the blessings and gifts we actually do have? Blessings and gifts of the spiritual kind (such as salvation, the Holy Spirit, fruits of the spirit) and the earthly kind, as well (such as friends, family, and a good church home)?

So often we fall easily into the "grass is greener" trap, assuming that what everyone else has is better than what we have.

The wife who longs for children, having one fertility treatment after another, might forget the blessing she has in a godly spouse, while the single woman at her church might happily trade anything in her life for marriage, children or not. The father out of work envies his well-paid Bible study leader who smiles and seems to have it all together, while that same Bible study leader tries to hide his pain over a decaying marriage and troubled son, and he envies the out-of-work father with his happy, loving family.

It's a difficult dilemma – just when you have what you think you want, you realize there's something else wrong or missing. Such is the condition of our broken, fallen, depraved hearts.

While we're here on this earth, we'll always long for something more than we have. Even when our desires are met, they are not as fulfilling as we imagined they would be. The ideas and dreams of next year's vacation are more vivid and exciting than the actual experience. The wafting smell of a delicious meal gives the impression that eating it will satisfy cravings, but after the first few bites, each following bite gives less pleasure than the one before until we're nearly sick of eating, no matter how great the meal. The same can be said of every single thing we desire, every single goal we drive towards, every single pleasure that hints to us that satisfaction and happiness is ours if we could only be, do, or have a particular thing.

Why is it that we can't be content?

Because our hearts were made for more. Our hearts were made for Jesus. ***Until Jesus is all we need, want, and long for, something will always be missing.***

So we long for health, wealth, and prosperity. We long for more sensational experiences. We seek physical pleasure that is temporary. We even design systems of theology that tell us God's ultimate plan for us is to experience all God has to offer in this temporary world we live in now.

But it takes only a cursory survey of those who achieve worldly success to show us that the things we desire don't satisfy us once we experience them.

There don't seem to be more smiles in the wealthy Western world than there are in the impoverished Sub-Saharan Africa or in third world Latin America. Frequently, those experiencing the greatest suffering are also those with the greatest joy.

Why is it that in scripture, we see some of the most faithful men and women experience the most suffering and struggle? Why did Elijah the prophet have to eat hundreds, if not thousands, of random bits-and-pieces of food, the meals brought by unclean birds?

The short answer is this: Our circumstances don't necessarily reflect the status of our faith. Period.

When I was a child, I thought of God as a sort of friendly

grandfather figure. He carried candy in His pocket, smiled at me, and just wanted me to be happy. As I've grown and matured, I understand more that God's ultimate purpose for me is to transform me...to make me more like Christ (Romans 8:28-29).

Our Americanized version of Christianity has in many ways, twisted the faith handed down to us through the ages. We have even hijacked the common Bible word, "blessed."

We feel "blessed" when something good happens. When the numbers turn up in our favor, when we get raises, cars, or anything else we might desire. But does this mean that we're less "blessed" when things aren't going in a direction that we hoped?

Let's take a quick look at how scripture can expand our understanding of what it means to be "blessed" by God. Here are a few examples of what God considers a blessed person to be.

Hold on to your seat, because it might not be what you're expecting. It may not be what you want to hear. Take a look at Matthew 5:1-12.

> Now when Jesus saw the crowds, he went up on a mountainside and sat down. His disciples came to him, and he began to teach them.
>
> He said:
>
> "Blessed are the poor in spirit,
> for theirs is the kingdom of heaven.
> Blessed are those who mourn,
> for they will be comforted.
> Blessed are the meek,
> for they will inherit the earth.
> Blessed are those who hunger and thirst for
> righteousness,

> for they will be filled.
> Blessed are the merciful,
> for they will be shown mercy.
> Blessed are the pure in heart,
> for they will see God.
> Blessed are the peacemakers,
> for they will be called children of God. Blessed
> are those who are persecuted because of
> righteousness,
> for theirs is the kingdom of heaven.
>
> "Blessed are you when people insult you, persecute you and falsely say all kinds of evil against you because of me.
>
> Rejoice and be glad, because great is your reward in heaven, for in the same way they persecuted the prophets who were before you.

Did you catch that? Look at the people Jesus called "blessed." Not a single mention of cash, cars, or house payments.

Instead, the "blessed" are these people: The poor in spirit. Those who mourn. The meek. Those who hunger and thirst for righteousness. The merciful. The pure in heart. The peacemakers. Those who are persecuted because of righteousness.

They don't exactly make the American success poster-child list, do they?

It gets worse. There's another sub-list that indicates an additional group whom Jesus called "blessed." Those who are not only persecuted for righteousness, but insulted and falsely accused as well.

What exactly does the word "blessed" mean? The ancient Greeks used it to describe a pleasant state of contentment, without stress or worry. They used the same word to describe how their gods didn't labor or experience stress.

The Old Testament writers used the concept of "blessed" to describe Eden. They also used it to describe the far off future, in the end of times – that beautiful day when the lion and lamb will nestle up together, the weapons of war will be made into harmless farm tools, when there will be no tears, when there will be no fear (Micah 4).

The Old Testament promise of future blessedness was not for the great, or powerful, or victorious. Not at all. The blessed life was a promise for God's people who were in that very moment in dire straits. This was a promise to those experiencing severe distress, to families and people who were suffering unimaginable devastation and anguish with zero hope except for God alone.

When Jesus the Messiah came into human history, He brought this "future" blessedness with Him, into the dusty byways of Galilee. By doing this, Jesus brings a sample of heaven into our lives in the here and now, while we are still in hunger, in our lowly estate, in our suffering, even as some of us are persecuted.

We say that Jesus "inaugurated" the future blessedness in His own ministry, and that His resurrection guarantees its success. For those of us who have been united with Christ in His death and resurrection, we can experience blessing – an incomparable sense of contentment, peace and spiritual belonging, even in the middle of the worst of our personal tragedies.[16]

Elijah was certainly blessed by God. But was he "blessed" by

16 James Leonard (PhD, Cambridge), history of the term "blessed" influenced by discussions between Dr. Leonard and the author, July 2015.

popular modern standards? He lived in the desert, in caves and desolate places, and ate meat and bread remnants from a bird. He had no home to speak of, few friends, and spent a significant amount of his life either delivering depressing judgments to kings who hated him, or running and hiding to save his life.

So what do blessings and financial hardship have to do with each other?

I'd like to suggest that maybe, just maybe, in all our sufferings and months out of work, the humiliation of second-rate clothing to wear to church and not enough money to pay for the kids' braces, and the exhaustion of a second job to pay the bills, *we are blessed.* We are more blessed than we ever thought possible, and we have more than we think we do. We have a high position, not a low one, because we know the provision of God on a daily basis. And as we work hard applying to hundreds of jobs, mourn the life we thought we'd have in exchange for the one He's given us, and long for the Bread of Life to fill us when we're tired and hungry from the late shift, we are blessed.

In some ways, we could have more than those living lives of ease and comfort, where God seems irrelevant because He simply isn't needed.

There are some verses about our needs that seem to run counter to what we see happen in the real world. One example is when Paul tells the Philippians that God will "meet all of our needs according to his glorious riches in Christ Jesus" (Philippians 4:19). But it doesn't take much searching to find examples of committed Christians who have died of starvation, or have even been killed because of their faith.

So does Philippians 4:19 promise that Christ followers will never have to experience suffering? Certainly not. Just a couple verses earlier, Paul writes, "I know how to live on almost nothing or with everything. I have learned the secret of living in every situation, whether it is with a full stomach or empty, with plenty or little. For I can do everything through Christ who gives me strength" (Philippians 4:12-13). In this context, it's clear that the needs God promises to meet for us are our spiritual needs.

God promises, no matter what hardship we find ourselves in, He will give us the strength to endure and stay faithful to Him.

Based on this, God *already* offers us everything we need.

That's impossible, you might think. We need food, and we have to have rent money, or a place to live. Aren't those needs? And He has promised to meet them, right?

Sure. For budgeting purposes, these things are definitely needs rather than luxuries and from the beginning of time God has been faithful to care and attend to the needs of the human race.

But what if, in the larger spiritual realm, even food and housing are not really needs after all?

What if the only true need we ever really had was for salvation, for peace with God on account of our sins? What if the only true need we ever had was our need for Jesus?

God has already met our greatest need.

We know from Scripture that Christians throughout the ages have suffered and died for their faith in unbelievable ways. Hebrews 11 lists a slew of tortures and death methods visited on the faithful. Where was God? Why did He not intervene, take away the punishment, and grant much-needed health, food, and life? Where was God when Job lay in the dust in agony, scratching himself with bits of broken pottery?

Did those people not have needs? God didn't appear to meet them.

Or did He?

What if their greatest need had already been met?

What if, two thousand years ago, God already provided for the greatest need anyone could ever have—from Moore, Oklahoma to Joplin, Missouri to Mount Carmel—with the blood of His own beloved Son, Jesus Christ?

After all, the human body was not created only for food, or safety, or even earthly life. We were created for fellowship with God. For eternity with Christ, glorifying and praising our Creator.

And before we'd even taken our first breath, God had already provided a way to reach out to us through the haze of sin and centuries to meet our deepest need.

For forgiveness of sins.

For Jesus Christ.

For peace with God, which no man on earth could purchase.

"'Come now, let us settle this,' says the Lord," wrote the prophet Isaiah. "Though your sins are like scarlet, I will make the white as snow" (Isaiah 1:18). And further, "He was pierced for our transgressions, he was crushed for our iniquities; the punishment that brought us peace was on him, and by his wounds we are healed" (Isaiah 53:5).

Friend, whatever financial hardship you're going through today is no secret to God. Trust the silence. Trust Him. He will meet all your needs. *He has already met all your needs.* Whether in life or death, in hunger and thirst, or in plenty, in times of good employment or leaner days, He is already there.

If you seek Him, you will find Him, even in your financial storm.

He will provide. He will provide Himself. He will never fail you.

To hear more about Hilarey Phillips's and Peter Friedlander's stories use the QR code below or go to www.WhereWasGod.com/book.

3

BROKEN RELATIONSHIPS

SHELTERING IN THE STORM

I said, "Oh, that I had the wings of a dove!
I would fly away and be at rest.
I would flee far away
and stay in the desert;
I would hurry to my place of shelter,
far from the tempest and storm..."
If an enemy were insulting me,
I could endure it;
if a foe were rising against me,
I could hide.
But it is you, a man like myself,

my companion, my close friend,
with whom I once enjoyed sweet fellowship
at the house of God,
as we walked about
among the worshipers.

- Psalm 55:5-8, 13-14 -

When I met Jason Head, he was working as the assistant editor on the movie, *Where Was God? Stories of Hope after the Storm.* This movie followed the lives of four main families who experienced tragedy and it chronicled their emotional and spiritual recovery after these life storms.

I helped gather stories to share in the film and I'd also been interviewed for the project as a local pastor. In my six hour interview, I talked about my relationship with my own father, with my Heavenly Father, and how my view of God's fatherhood impacts my spiritual growth. More specifically, I was asked questions about how tragedy can drive you to become closer to God and family rather than drive you away. This real life documentary from real people sharing authentic stories about God and how they found Him in tragedy impacted everyone who worked on the film.

Jason's job, along with the rest of the editing team, was to pour through more than 160 hours of interviews, second by second, to help cut down these hours into a succinct 90 minutes that could be shared in movie theaters. One single story line linked all of these real life stories.

By the time Jason and I met, I had taken over as the Executive Producer.

Prior to this project, I was not a film professional. The impressive title of Executive Producer only means that I helped raise money by continually asking everyone I knew for donations. It seems that the film industry has found an effective way to attract donors, investors, or fundraisers. Just give them a super cool name and put them in the credits of a movie! I swallowed that bait completely.

About midway through the post-production (editing), I received a message through one of the other producers who said, "Jason Head wants to meet with you and talk about the fatherhood of God and to tell you his story."

I was intrigued and I'm always interested in hearing someone's story.

Jason, 27 years old at that time, told me that growing up, he didn't have a single relationship that wasn't broken. His mom was a severe alcoholic and suffering from depression. Jason told me his dad was "an alcoholic, liar, cheater, child abuser, and most of all a very proud man."

Over the next couple of hours, Jason described a sinister haze of beatings, domestic violence, rape, drunkenness, and sexual abuse, coming to a head when his mother stabbed his dad and ran away with Jason and his siblings. Then he and his brothers and sisters suffered through divorce, custody battles, and violence. His sister sold drugs and went to jail; the rest of his brothers remained estranged, in jail, or lost in their own darkness of pain. His connections with almost everyone in his family were deeply damaged, and according to Jason, none of them really share the closeness people think of as "family."

As a child, like most kids, Jason assumed his life was "normal."

"I didn't realize my relationships within my family were messed up until I was in middle school," says Jason, "after my dad had pounded on my face for about four years. In high school I realized how messed up I was. I was too scared to get close to anyone, but I always had a yearning for someone to know that I existed."

Jason admits the origin of the brokenness in his life came directly from his parents. At least at first. "As I became older I started to retaliate," he said. "And I did throw fuel on the fire in just about every relationship I had."

In his early years, Jason had occasionally been to church and camps, but he didn't personally know the love of God until after the death of his father. As he watched his dad beg for water on his death bed, Head said something inside him changed.

"I knew at that moment even the most frightening man I had encountered was vulnerable to death," he recalls.

Jason's dad's passing was followed by the quick and unexpected death of a young friend. These two experiences sparked a season that changed Jason's life drastically.

In an experience that reminds me of Paul's New Testament conversion in Acts 9, Jason believes he heard directly from God at a funeral. This funeral was for a young man who Jason had partied with previously. The dangerous lifestyle along with a new understanding of life's fragility was what God used to draw Jason to Himself.

When the crowd was asked if anyone wanted to share anything, Jason stood to share memories about his friend. When he did, he was immediately overwhelmed by a sense of his need for God. He was surrounded by friends who knew of his drug abuse, his party lifestyle, his fighting, and his brokenness. Jason talked openly about what God was doing in his heart, right in those moments. He publicly confessed his brokenness. He expressed his need for God's love, grace, and forgiveness. He even shared with the crowd that they too were in need of Jesus.

"I started to cry," recalls Jason. "I knew from that moment forward that God was bigger than me, and Jesus was more than my definition of love could fathom. I guess you could say God initiated a relationship with me, and I couldn't deny Him. I had to trust Him. That moment in His presence changed my whole life."

"After that, I threw what clothes I had in a trash bag, gave everything I had away, and moved in with the Christians I'd just met," says Jason. "And I've been serving the Lord ever since."

And while life still has its ups and downs for Head, and plenty of wreckage from the past, Jason has come a long way from the shattered relationships of his youth.

"When it comes to broken relationships, God can fix up more than we can mess up," he says. "God is love, and love is the only thing that brings our hearts into relationship, covenant, and peace. He is always before me, ministering the truth of his love, setting up situations and moments of divine healing. He is my joy."

It wasn't long after he decided to follow Christ that Jason got a job working on the *Where Was God?* movie. This season ushered in some new relationships, new change, and healing.

"Working on the *'Where Was God?'* project allowed me to meet Steven Earp and hear his father-and-son relationships with God," says Jason. "I'd definitely never wanted to see God as my dad because my definition of a father did not match the indescribable relationships I found with God. I realize what a father should look like now. Now I can bless my children with love."

Jason has come to realize that his earthly father was not merely a "bad person." "He was defective simply because he did not know God," Jason says. "My heart hurts for him, but I don't hurt because of him anymore."

And that pain is what drove Jason straight to God.

Many of us can identify with Jason and his fear of getting close to people, and as Jason put it, the "yearning for someone to know that I exist."

There are few things in life that shake us more than strained or shattered relationships. The loneliness can be agonizing, frightening.

From the moment we're born, we crave touch, smiles, speech, love. Almost everything we do, everything we become, everything we are in our unfolding lives hinges on relationships and how we're connected to those around us. We fill books and web albums with photos. We send letters and care packages and flowers and emails. We spend thousands of hours on the phone or send tens of thousands of text messages. We either agonize or exult over the various shades of relational nuances, whether or not she's angry, whether or not I used the right words in that discussion, why he's suddenly cold, or if she glanced my way on purpose or not. Every. Single. Day.

Stop anybody on the street and ask them either 1) what they're talking or texting about or 2) what music they're listening to on their iPod, and there's a good chance it'll be about relationships. Love, joy, angst, depression, jealousy, anger, and every shade in between. We alternately struggle and rejoice over relationships with parents, friends, children, and co-workers. And the subtle turning of one can shape our entire day. Maybe, even, our entire lives.

In light of all our toils, poetry, heartbreak, songs, and smiles, the Almighty might seem to those who don't know Him as somewhat detached from it all. "The man upstairs," people flippantly call Him, as if He's "up there" and we're "down here," and He's somewhat clueless (or careless) about what happens to us. God is depicted in comic form as a white-bearded grandfather, smiling in benevolence—if not senility when He's not throwing out lightning bolts on unsuspecting victims.

"God?" you might be thinking. "He doesn't understand relationships the way I do."

God, it seems, has a narrow, stuffy, old-fashioned view of what brings relational happiness. So much so that His ways appear almost an embarrassment in our modern era of personal "freedom." Heterosexual marriage only? Believing that "Jesus is the only way?" No sex before marriage? Honoring parents? Letting go of married sons and daughters? Leave and cleave? Disciplining children while they're young? Forgiving? Staying married?

Who is this God, anyway? "If He were in my shoes, He'd give different advice." He'd feel, He'd bleed, He'd weep. He'd cry out in agony and frustration and experience the sting of rejection, of betrayal, of unrequited love.

But that's just it. He has.

God, the living God of the Bible, has walked in human skin, laughed with human friends, and been nailed to a cross by haters and friends-turned-enemies. No one on earth has experienced the depth of pain and betrayal that Jesus the God-in-flesh did, and no one has ever loved—or been loved—more deeply.

The Bible, in fact, is not a dry collection of laws and rules and history. It's a love story. A story of God's love for us, for the humanity He created, full of poetry, songs, and intimate, deeply moving stories. Some of his analogies read like lover's quarrels, begging His beloved to come back to reality and love Him like she used to.

What is it that's weighing your heart down today? What has broken the innermost parts of you? What bitter words ring in your ears, year after year, and what do you struggle most to forgive and release?

It might seem impossible, but God can still work even in the worst of situations. I know because He's done it not just for kings like David, but for normal folks like Jason Head. And for me. And for more people than I can list here in one book.

But it isn't easy, and it's almost never a pretty process.

Consider, for starters, the pain and strained relationships that

Jason Head still experiences with certain people in his extended family. Jason loves the Lord, but that doesn't take away the difficult interactions he still has to face, or the scars he bears from the pain of his childhood and turbulent teen years. It doesn't fix the choices and consequences that he still lives with today.

"Tempest and storm," the psalmist and king David calls it—the mess of brokenness and hateful words. The slammed doors and icy silence. The divorce, the weeping, the custody arrangements.

And some, like the verses in Psalm 55 penned by David, reflect the utter devastation of a trusted friend who turns the knife in betrayal.

For God, you see, has experienced it all, and long before we did. Our feeble jealousies and quarrels pale in comparison to the emotions felt by the Maker of all relationships, the Initiator of intimacy, the Creator of love.

And David, the shepherd boy turned king of Israel, is a shimmering biblical hero known as "a man after God's own heart." If anybody knew broken relationships, it was David, the shepherd and musician who captured the hearts of nearly everyone who met him. Warrior, fugitive, husband, father, lover of God. The boy who stared down the giant with a sling and five smooth stones. Even centuries later, we still whisper prayers penned by the poet-king, where he poured out his heart to God.

And one thing we know about David is that he hurt a lot. David was betrayed, hated unjustly, and forced to flee through the wilderness to save his own life.

David's complex relationships and players run the gamut of nearly every combination possible: a wholeheartedly devoted friend until death (Jonathan), a mentor turned enemy (Saul), an enemy turned friend (Abigail), a loving wife who came to despise him (Michal), an estranged beloved son (Absalom), relatives who despised and mocked him (older brothers), a father who thought he wasn't fit to be counted as a son (Jesse), a rapist son killed by another son (Amnon), a sexually abused daughter (Tamar), a loyal subject he had murdered (Uriah), a woman with whom he had an illicit affair (Bathsheba), a son born of an adulterous relationship who became a blessing (Solomon), and an act of sin against God that brought devastating consequences.

David, if he lived today, would be the most-watched TV reality show star on the networks.

His life reads almost like a soap opera script: tragedy after heartbreak after sweeping romance. He wept, raged, implored, fumbled, made rash decisions, begged, and consoled. Few characters in the Bible have ever had as many intimate thoughts, emotions, and struggles between people recorded as David, and they are filled with such depth and beauty.

David might understand some of the pain that Jason Head went through.

Coming to Christ isn't a magic wand that makes everything in our lives perfect. And of course not, for it was never intended to do that.

We can all name those difficult people—the ones who have hurt us, betrayed us, and continue to inflict harm instead of good. The people we wish we didn't have to deal with. And, maddeningly, the people we can't seem to get rid of.

So how exactly can we find God when our storm is relational? When our hearts are broken along with the shattered dreams of relationships? When someone, who used to be or should be in our lives, no longer is? Because of sin, perhaps theirs or perhaps mine? Here are some principles that can help us meet the Lord in the midst or even the aftermath of our broken relationships.

1. FOCUS FIRST ON WHAT YOU ALONE CAN CONTROL.

The only thing I can control is my own internal and external response to the struggle.

In our family, we've been intentional about what we call our "family culture." We never felt that good relationships, experiences, and memories would just *happen*, so we make great efforts to do some things on purpose. We rely on common values to unite us. We call that our family culture.

Part of our family culture is that we live by certain mottos. I'm not sure where I initially picked it up, but since our kids were tiny, we taught them, "You can accept responsibility or you can place blame, but you can't do both."

The idea is to accept personal responsibility for whatever happens in life.

I can only grow through things when I own my role in them.

So is God in control, or am I responsible for what happens? The answer is... *yes*. Both, actually. God's sovereignty doesn't dismiss our need for accepting personal responsibility at all. In fact, spiritual salvation is all about relationship—namely how we enter into a relationship with a holy God in the first place. And it requires enough humility to admit we're broken and unworthy of Him!

I can only change what I take responsibility for. I can only grow when I press into my own culpability.

God starts changing me when I acknowledge my part in my own brokenness.

In my own life, for example, I contributed to most of the relational storms I've experienced. The same can be said about David and his poor choices.

One of the best examples of David's need for personal change is found in 2 Samuel 12, where the prophet Nathan confronts David of his grossly blatant sin in lusting after Bathsheba (a married woman) and having an affair with her, and then having her husband killed to cover it up.

David seems to have become complacent in his position as king – even arrogant. Nathan's words shook him up.

> Then Nathan said to David, "You are the man! This is what the Lord, the God of Israel, says: 'I anointed you king over Israel, and I delivered you from the hand of Saul. I gave your master's house to you, and your master's wives into your arms. I gave you all Israel and Judah. And if all this had been too little, I would have given you even more. Why did you despise the word of the lord by doing what is evil in his eyes? ... Now, therefore, the sword will never depart from your house, because you despised me and took the wife of Uriah the Hittite to be your own'...
>
> Then David said to Nathan, *"I have sinned against the LORD"* (2 Samuel 2:7-13).

It's clear from the Psalms that Nathan's revelation of David's guilt had crushed David's heart. Of course David recognized all along that he had openly plotted – and committed – grave sins. What is striking is that it took so long for it to bother his conscience. Had he initially rationalized his actions to himself, figuring that since he'd become king he had unlimited powers? Or had he simply gotten out of tune with God's will in his life until he no longer listened to his conscience at all?

The Bible isn't clear about why David committed such shocking sins, nor why it took so long and a visit from the prophet for him to catch on. But the good news is that he did, and his honest confession helped him to turn from his sin and ask for forgiveness before it was too late.

Sometimes a broken relationship or two is all we need to help us make an urgently needed course correction.

Has it taken a falling out with a good friend to help you realize your fault in a matter? Or how about an argument with your husband or wife to bring up some of your attitudes that aren't fitting for a child of God? That one nagging, needling co-worker who gives you practice with patience, kindness, and forgiveness?

OUR CRUSHED SPIRITS CAN BE USED FOR GOOD

"To us, broken things are despised as worthless, but God can take what has been broken and remake it into something better, something that He can use for His glory," says one article on biblical relationships. "Broken things and broken people are the result of sin. Yet God sent his Son, who was without sin, to be broken so that we might be healed. On the night before He died, Jesus broke the bread and said, 'This is my body, which is broken for you.' Without the broken body of Jesus, we could not be made whole."

This brokenness, writes the author, opens us up for God to change and mold us in better ways. When we surrender to Him, it brings new dependence on him, and transformation from the person we were to the person God wants us to be. [17]

The key is to look for the area where we so desperately need personal change, and then to confess it to God, to the other party, and to learn from our mistakes.

Even if it's just a drop in the ocean of the other person's offenses, it will make us better people if we confess it and learn from it anyway.

We know that when we do this, God can bring good out of any situation, even the most fractured of relationships. Look no further than the book of Genesis and the story of Joseph, whose jealous half-brothers sold him into slavery in Egypt. After years of Joseph's servitude, imprisonment, and subsequent rise to fame, Joseph's brothers came back into the picture again: this time coming to buy food for their families back in famine-parched Israel.

Joseph, now a prominent ruler in Pharaoh's court, tested his brothers to find out if their hard hearts had changed, and when he determined they had, received them all back with weeping and forgiveness.

"You intended to harm me, but God intended it for good," said Joseph in Genesis 50:20, "to accomplish what is now being done, the saving of many lives."

This is the nature of the God we serve. So many times we can look back over our lives and see that what others might have intended to hurt us, God turns around and uses for our good, our growth and for His glory.

Everything difficult in our lives can be used for good by the Lord, if we let Him.

---

17 "What does the Bible say about brokenness?" in gotquestions.org, undated, (http://www.gotquestions.org/Bible-brokenness.html#ixzz30a50qDrM, accessed July 18, 2015).

Trust Him to bring out the best in any situation, in any failed relationship, even when it seems impossible, because Scripture says, "nothing is impossible with God."

He will show you where you need sifting, where you need change, and help you become a better man or woman, fit for the kingdom of God.

But sometimes there's more to our stories. What if my relational brokenness is due to circumstances beyond my control? In the case of Jason Head, for example, one can hardly lay fault at the feet of a battered youth.

We're not always to blame. Jason Head, an innocent child, wasn't responsible for his difficult family circumstances. David didn't ask to be passed over as a son or targeted by King Saul in a jealous rage. Both of them were innocent victims; neither of them needed to "confess sin" or take responsibility for the other party's evil actions.

None of us asked for the wounds that came during our tender childhood years, or for the hurt caused by foes with malicious intent. We didn't ask to be bullied, or beaten, or lied about. And God knows all about our pain. As a pastor and a man who's been hurt, I still know one thing is true: even if I have zero culpability in a relational storm, I will only be able to meet the Lord by committing to change and grow through the recovery process. Why? I'm the only person I can control.

I can change my attitude about the problems. I can forgive. I can confess and seek reconciliation when possible. Personal change has to be the first step.

But even when we're innocent, that same principle is still true. We are still responsible for our own actions.

How? Not in the ways you might think! Not by admitting fault that really isn't there, or by imagining some sin on your part that you didn't commit. Not by "trying to understand the other person" or explaining away his or her sins.

None of this.

The crucial way that we can still take responsibility for ourselves and our actions when we're innocent and wounded is this: *By letting God mold us in response to the sin of the other person.*

Let that sink in. Don't miss this. It's powerful. Even when we've been deeply wronged, *especially* when we've been deeply wronged, God can use this pain to grow us in Him.

Because when we open ourselves up to God's work, even with our wounds, even in our grief, He will begin to heal us, to change us, and to bring us to a special, consecrated place where He can use us more fully.

Maybe He'll use us to comfort others. Maybe He'll open our spiritual eyes so that we can teach people to know more of His great heart. Maybe He'll do far more than we can imagine if we open ourselves, wounded as we are, to His work, and trust Him.

Trust Him, like a hurt child trusts the gentle hands of a loving father, the kind of father many of us have only dreamed of having. The kind of father who would love you, not abuse you; the kind of father who would die for you, not destroy you.

Because your loving Heavenly Father knows your hurts. He knows you tried, over and over again, to offer peace and got nothing but a slap in the face. He knows you were abused, or beaten, or seduced against your will.

If you let God, He will use even that for your betterment and for His glory.

He did it for Jason Head, when his earthly father left him battered and broken on the inside and outside. Jason himself confesses, "When I look at my son now, I realize he is very important. I didn't always see him as important. I abandoned him for the first seven years of his life because of my thinking. Whether or not my father meant to make me feel this way, I always felt I was there to serve him. I felt he tolerated me more than he desired my existence. That feeling of 'unimportance' has affected every one of my relationships."

Recently, though, something has shifted inside Jason. Something big.

"My wife and I went to get an ultrasound of our new child a few weeks ago and it changed my life," he says. "Something happened to my heart when I saw the little baby moving. I realized this little person needs me. I have never felt anything as unique as that. I left the hospital remembering being homeless and hungry when I was 17. God took that feeling of abandonment and replaced it with a boldness to fulfill the call of fatherhood. I know now I have to pour myself out and give our children spiritual guidance on a path of consistent fellowship with God."

God did it for David, when all the running and hiding from King Saul left him exhausted. God showed him a new source of strength: Himself. In the now-famous Psalm 23 David writes the following:

"The Lord is my shepherd, I lack nothing.
He makes me lie down in green pastures,
he leads me beside quiet waters,
he refreshes my soul.
He guides me along the right paths
for his name's sake.
Even though I walk
through the darkest valley,
I will fear no evil,
for you are with me."

As David faced down giants and ran for his life, he learned to trust the Lord as tenderly as a sheep looks to his shepherd for comfort and protection. He let God quiet his heart, refresh his wounded soul, and stand by him in the darkest valley.

God will do the same for you.

God can bring good out of even the worst of sins and offenses, whether or not you were at fault.

Just one caution: That is not to say, of course, that every relationship can be restored.

Jason Head's father died without making any kind of reconciliation or apology to his son. And no matter how hard David tried to make things good with King Saul, he could not. Saul was bent on destroying David's life out of jealousy and fear, and even God's rejection of Saul as king didn't convince him to stop.

David's relationship with his son Absalom ended in grief and death, with no chance for them to reconcile. Even David's first wife, Michal, changed over the years from loving David to hating him, and her last words in the Bible record her disgust and rejection. There is no evidence of reconciliation between David and Michal for the rest of their lives, and they never had children together.

David certainly had his share of faults in his large extended family, but not everything was his fault. And not everything is yours.

"As much as it depends on you," says the Apostle Paul, "live at peace with all men" (Romans 12:18).

As much as it depends on you pray for the one you've fallen out of fellowship with. *As much as it depends on you* offer yourself to talk through what went wrong, and admit your fault in the problem, even if it's a small thing. *As much as it depends on you* refuse to gossip or treat the one who's hurt you with retaliation. Forgive. Go the extra mile. Be willing to start again.

As much as it depends on you, because you're the only one you can control. Do your part, and leave the rest in God's hands.

2. LEAVE *YOURSELF* IN GOD'S HANDS

Remember, even if you've done everything possible, the relationship may still remain broken. It doesn't all depend on us. There are many factors involved in the complex business of restoring relationships, and the other person may or may not respond.

Ultimately God—not us—is sovereign over relationships.

Actually, some relationships may need to end. The unhealthy friendship that's draining you dry? You might need to let it go. The abusive, angry boyfriend who keeps your stomach in knots? Get out of it now, while you still can. The man or woman tempting you to leave your spouse? Cut them out of your life and don't look back.

The spiteful relatives that want nothing more than to see you fail? It's time to emotionally move on. Don't give someone permission to control your heart. Spend your time in better company if you can. When you do find yourself at unavoidable family events, take the high road. Be kind, be loving, be polite and use the abrasive interactions of others to develop your inner life by loving them even more deeply.

If you're experiencing relational stress with your spouse, seek help now. Run, don't walk, to a pastor or Christian counselor's office, even if you go alone. Fast. Pray. Beg God to bring healing to your marriage, and control the part you can control: yourself and your reactions, trusting God to bring good to you even through your pain.

If you're being physically abused by your spouse, this is more than a simple "relational problem," it's a serious, life-threatening danger.

And it's a crime. You must get help—and now—whether by calling the police or a domestic abuse hotline, or simply telling the truth to your pastor or close friend. Or preferably all of the above!

Above all, "Hate what is evil, and cling to what is good" (Romans 12:9).

And if a splintered relationship with a friend, co-worker, or relative has enough good left in it that it's still a blessing and a benefit, and you're both willing to work on it, you might be ready for a miracle. A resurrection. Because God's in that business, too.

3. REALIZE THAT GOD CAN RAISE DEAD RELATIONSHIPS.

You may have heard the story of Abraham, of how he offered his son Isaac to God as a sacrifice, and God provided a ram instead. And Abraham, says the book of Hebrews, was able to offer Isaac because he "reasoned that God was able to raise the dead." (Hebrews 11:19)

But Abraham wasn't the only one who trusted God to raise the dead. Acts 2:31 says that David also believed God's resurrection promise: "Seeing what was to come, he spoke of the resurrection of the Messiah, that he was not abandoned to the realm of the dead, nor did his body see decay."

God gave David the uncanny spiritual ability to look through time, so to speak, and to recognize spiritual truths about life and death, about Jesus the Messiah, and how he'd eventually triumph over death.

Raising the dead is a hallmark of the divine, from David and Abraham's affirmations to Christ-like prototypes of prophets Elijah and Elisha to the miracles of Jesus and his disciples.

If God is able to resurrect flesh and blood, He can certainly resurrect broken relationships. The body of Christ has seen loveless marriages restored, estranged friendships healed, and divided parents and children brought together again.

David himself was brought back into fellowship with God after he repented of his sin, following punishment and sharp condemnation by the prophet Nathan. What had been fractured was then healed, and what had expired now moved with fresh life.

The apostle Peter was also reinstated into the ministry after he denied knowing Jesus, and he went on to be one of the greatest apostles, leaders, and martyrs for the faith the world has ever known.

Bunny Yekzaman, a chaplain, wife, and mother of four, can testify to God's ability to raise even the worst of relationships from the dead. After her father sexually abused her as a child, their relationship drifted apart to the point where she no longer even knew where he lived. As a committed follower of Jesus, Bunny longed to communicate her forgiveness for him, as well as her thankfulness for him taking her to church when she was younger—the one thing that stood out to her as a blessing. After all, it was through church that she'd become a Christian and received a call to missions.

Even if Bunny and her dad were never able to enjoy a close, healthy relationship, she wanted to thank him. But how would she contact him after so many years apart?

One day, Bunny received an email from someone named Sharon.

"Sharon? That's my dad's wife," Bunny said. "I couldn't wait to open it and read it, thinking I was finally going to be able to tell dad 'thank you,' but within moments my heart began to break, and the tears began to fall. Dad had died three weeks earlier of lung cancer while I was on the mission field. He didn't want anyone to know he was dying."

Amazingly, though, that wasn't the end. Bunny met with Sharon a few days later and asked, through tears, whether her dad had changed.

"Then she spoke words that made my heart smile. Sharon told me this: 'For the last two years of your dad's life, he got it. He finally understood that God could forgive him, and he went around telling as many people as he could about Jesus,'" recalls Bunny. "My tears fell even harder at this point. Wow, Dad got it. He truly gained a relationship with God."

"Oh, how I would have loved to see that!" she says. "But as the months and years passed, I have thought so much about all this, and I realized that in the moment my dad gave his life to Christ, we now have a very special connection: the Holy Spirit.

"Dad may not be here with us on this earth, but I know one day I will be with him in Heaven where all the pain, ugliness, and garbage of our past will be gone, and we will spend eternity together praising the Lord."

4. UNDERSTAND THE NATURE OF FORGIVENESS.

Any time we discuss forgiveness and relationships, we must also mention a caveat: Reuniting isn't always a good thing.

A lot of Christian material can make it sound like forgiveness automatically equals a close relationship or a strange amnesia toward past wrongs, but that isn't always the case. While we can forgive even without an apology from the offender, that kind of one-sided forgiveness mainly sets us free and puts us in a right relationship with Christ and heals things in our own hearts. This doesn't necessarily fix the relationship.

Some relationships should not be pursued, even for restoration. Chronic abusers, for example, can certainly be forgiven, but allowing them to freely continue to abuse without recompense would be enabling and dangerous, not forgiving. Without proper laws and punishments there'd be no penal system at all—no jails, no fines—we'd just "let them all go" in the name of "love" and "forgiveness" so they can continue to rape, steal, and kidnap children at will. Can you imagine? That's not love and forgiveness. That's chaos.

Furthermore, in many cases of abuse, it's simply better for there to be no contact at all, ever, between the two parties so that the wounded person can heal. Boundaries (including no-contact boundaries in some circumstances) are healthy and can be healing. The Bible never says we need to be best buddies with sexual abusers or violent ex-boyfriends. That wouldn't be helpful, and it certainly wouldn't promote healing.

Healing comes when we are able to truly forgive our offenders as we have been forgiven. Nothing anyone could ever do to us can equal the debt we owe Christ, or the great debt we have been forgiven as children of God.

True healing comes when we are able to release our offender into the hands of God, and most importantly, to be honest about our full range of emotions before God and receive the healing that He offers. Forgiveness is basically emotionally letting go of someone's neck and no longer holding them responsible for the well-being of your inner life and happiness.

Forgiveness, friends, is not for the faint of heart.

And this is why forgiveness, contrary to popular belief, doesn't mean watering down what a person has done. It doesn't mean "seeing things from her perspective," or "thinking how he must have been feeling," or coming to the conclusion that "what he did wasn't really that bad after all."

It's not about making excuses for him or for her. It's not about "she was tired," or "he had a rough childhood."

While these kind-sounding thoughts might be extremely helpful to a victim's healing process, or perhaps the restoration of the relationship, they are *not* forgiveness!

Forgiveness takes the whole unadulterated, undiluted sin in all of its unholy ugliness and lays it at Christ's feet for his love to cover. It does not need to be explained, excused, or swept partially under the rug to be forgiven. His love is powerful and complete enough to cover any sin, no matter how terrible, without exception.

When I truly understood this, it was life-changing for me.

What a radical principle, that God's love and grace is enough to cover *anything* anyone has ever done to me without making excuses for the offender!

Sometimes I think people try to "explain" a person's sins away in order to make it seem less offensive, because we doubt (perhaps on an unconscious level) that God's love is really strong enough to cover the whole offense, and therefore we must "help Him out" by making the sin seem a little better than it is.

And if we go that route, we might feel pity, or sympathy, or some subtle thoughts that temporarily assuage our anger, but we are mistaken if we think those things contribute to forgiveness. No! *Forgiveness has nothing to do with how we feel!*

Forgiveness has everything to do with the blood of Jesus, which is powerful enough to take away all sin!

If we miss this important point, we might think we've forgiven, when indeed we haven't. And we may muddle through years and years of smoldering struggles to press down the offenses, to push them back in the box and slam the lid, when they don't want to be slammed. Because they haven't been heard.

Your frustrations and hurts need to be heard, because they're expressing the truth about what you're feeling.

"Understanding" this or that is not necessary. Feeling sympathy is not necessary. Only Christ is necessary, and only He can fully forgive and release complete forgiveness that covers the entire sin, because He is the only one who's able to take that on.

If you doubt, look no further than the Psalms, many of them which were penned by none other than King David. His psalms reflect brutal honesty, anger, disappointment, pain and even jealousy, but by the last stanza of each psalm, he expresses genuine confidence in God, if not praise. He never sugarcoated sin or ignored his emotions. No, he cried out to God in complete openness, and "the man after God's own heart" found healing and peace.

Forgiveness is a spiritual discipline intended by God to help bring us healing, and also to help us keep our own hearts right. For not one of us, if our sins were weighed by a holy God, could remain standing.

"Does she deserve forgiveness? Is he worthy of being forgiven?" These thoughts might go through our mind, but perhaps there are better questions for us to ask. It's easy to point the finger and find guilt in others, when in fact we are all guilty of different kinds of sin.

We might ask ourselves instead: "What does God want to do in my heart as I wrestle through the process of forgiving? Am I enough like God to be worthy of acting as the judge, jury, and executioner in my heart as it relates to this person's sins against me? Can I continue growing in my walk with Christ if I don't press in and work through the difficult tasks of forgiving?"

Because His forgiveness is there and available to cover every sin that you, I, or anyone else could ever commit.

Do you think forgiveness is easy? No. In fact, it will require some degree of suffering on your part. It's swallowing the feeling of joy at the notion of seeing the other party suffer for his sins against you. It's forever internalizing and processing the hurt rather than lashing out at her, because of what you perceive she deserves.

But it's more than worth it for the peace we have with God, and in our spirit, as a result.

Micah Moody, a wife and mother of three, whose home was destroyed in the Moore tornado can testify to the healing work that both forgiveness and tough love has brought into her life. From her teens Micah became involved in drugs and alcohol, eventually coming to a place where her mother sent out of the house. She arranged an apartment for Micah to take care of herself, but it didn't work.

"I fell flat on my face," says Micah. "I was even homeless for a while. The second time I came crawling back to my mom, she kicked me out with no financial assistance when I got back into my old ways. 'You're not willing to live under the rules of the home. You're bringing destruction to this home.'"

The words hit hard for Micah, and the third time she went back home, she knew this was it. "I was starting to go down that path again, and I knew my mom was never going to let me come back if I didn't get my act together. She had to be tough on me, and she didn't enable me.

While it was painful for her, mom knew what would happen. If she let me stay home I would destroy myself."

Micah went to Alcoholics Anonymous, where she met her husband, James. Interestingly enough, Micah used her mom's "tough love" and forgiveness strategies when James relapsed several times over the years.

"One thing that was key to me being able to forgive James is that he fully acknowledged his wrongdoing, just like David did (in the Bible), with a very detailed repentance, and he has always been man enough to come back and take responsibility for what he's done," she says. "It's one of the things we try to teach our kids, to take responsibility and be accountable and have the maturity to say 'I failed.' We want them to know that they don't have to be perfect, and that maybe they'll look back and see that I've been loyal to James even though it's been painful."

Giving grace to others is costly.

Micah says it this way, "For me, being gracious costs me my own thoughts and feelings. I have to leave those behind and go God's way. It's painful. It hurts. It's agonizing sometimes. But that's exactly what Jesus meant when he talked about counting the cost. So many of us are not prepared to sit down and count that cost because we want it to be a fairytale."

The truth is that everything costs, including unforgiveness. It can eat away at your heart, causing you to be bitter, angry, and hate-filled. And God knows that when we release it all to Him, He will make something greater out of it than we could possibly imagine at the time.

In Micah and James' case, mutual forgiveness—and the rewards of remaining faithful through hard times—have blessed them with a special marriage, three beautiful children, and a unique testimony that equips them to encourage people who are dealing with the hardest issues life can throw at them. They know because they've been there, and they've found God faithful through it all.

Micah says Psalm 62:5 has been her lifeline: "Yes, my soul finds rest in God; my hope comes from Him."

Because our hope comes from Him, and not from people who will eventually let us down.

"James and I both bring brokenness into this marriage" she says. "We're all broken people, and everybody who comes together is broken in some way. We're whole in Christ but we're still struggling with the flesh."

But that struggle, says Micah, is where the gospel and Christ's love become so clear.

"My mom loved me more than how her parenting looked to me," says Micah. "When you have to love to the point where you have to be hurtful—that's the perfect love that Jesus displayed on the cross—selfless, painful love."

5. KNOW THAT GOD CAN HEAL OUR PAIN.

What do we do with all of those broken pieces and the ache of harsh words or actions? Give them to the Lord.

Repeatedly in Scripture God is referred to as a healer, binder of wounds, strength of the broken, the lifter of our heads. In fact, one of God's specific names is Jehovah Rapha: "the Lord our Healer."

There is no grief He cannot shoulder, and no pain He cannot heal. Even the worst of offenses can eventually be reconciled in our hearts by the healing love of Jesus.

"The Lord is close to the broken-hearted," says Psalm 34:18, "and saves those who are crushed in spirit." Yet another deep thought from David, when he was on the run from King Saul's raging anger. Even then David found healing and peace in the Lord.

Through wisdom and growth from the relationships we've damaged already, God can teach us how to be better friends, better Christians, better mothers and fathers, better husbands and wives, better sons and daughters and brothers and sisters. Like Micah and James Moody, like Jason Head, like Bunny Yekzaman, and like the great King David, we can go on in life and become better people because of our brokenness. We gain understanding, sympathy, and mercy.

6. RELATIONSHIPS ARE WORTH IT, EVEN THOUGH THEY REQUIRE SACRIFICE.

It's clear that even good relationships come with a cost, and in some cases a great cost.

It's one of the most unforgettable friendships in all of history: Jonathan, son of Saul, King of Israel, and David, the young hero that Jonathan's father hated. David and Jonathan persevered in a close and joyful friendship despite David's persecution and eventual flight for his life. Jonathan even saved David's life from his own father, and vowed loyalty to him even over his own family.

In fact, Jonathan's loyalty to David was so strong that he sacrificed his own kingship for the sake of David. As the son of Saul, he would have been next in line to wear the crown had this young upstart from Jesse's clan not shown up. But Jonathan recognized the anointing of David as God's candidate for the position, over his father, and even over himself. So he did everything in his power to help David escape his father's rage and help him obtain the throne.

David, too, suffered for his dedication to Jonathan, mourning the death of his dearest friend in battle, and he spent the remainder of his time as king looking for relatives of Jonathan to bless in honor of his dear friend. At a time when new kings systematically hunted down and slaughtered relatives of previous royalty to ensure the throne, David chose to bless Jonathan's family. No doubt, David also frequently wept for the loss of his friend periodically through the years.

Wouldn't it have been easier for David to leave his painful relationship with Jonathan behind and find a more suitable friend? A friend from the same "camp," perhaps, rather than from Saul's line? Wouldn't it have been more expedient for Jonathan to leave David behind and cling to the throne for himself?

But David—and Jonathan, especially—chose the harder, more painful road.

If you asked either of them, though, they'd probably say it was the *right* road. And it was worth it. They went to their graves committed to the friendship they'd pledged themselves to as young men.

For God-given friendship is always right, and always a blessing. Both David and Jonathan have the weighty accomplishment of having loved another more than himself, of having stood by another's side when the going got tough, and of having completed the hard task with honor, which makes them better people in anyone's book.

Sometimes, as in the case of David and Jonathan, the right relationship choice *will* be the harder one.

Ask the woman who stands by her husband's side as he's diagnosed with a debilitating disease that will leave him unable to provide for their family. Ask the teen who risks everything to speak up and to get her anorexic friend the help she needs.

Relationships require more of us than we may want to give at first.

The thing is, Jesus anticipates this very dilemma in Matthew 10:37: "Anyone who loves their father or mother more than me is not worthy of me; anyone who loves their son or daughter more than me is not worthy of me."

It sounds counterintuitive, but Jesus knew that following Him would get hard. He knew that we would face pressure to abandon our faith, to give up, to go back to being the people we used to be. The path to godliness, though, is not found in ease, but in faithfulness no matter what. It's not found in comfort, but in giving up comfort for the Kingdom, and for others, even for our enemies. It's not found in lack of effort, but in steadfast determination at personal cost.

In fact, no one has ever given up more for love than Jesus, who sacrificed His own life and suffered unbelievable, undeserved torture and rejection, for one purpose: to help us find peace with God.

Our earthly relationships, along with anything else positive in this world, are really just images of what our existence will be when one day we are able to see Christ face to face. What goodness we experience here and now is barely a scent of what is to come.

So why are relationships so difficult? Relationships require sacrifice. Relationships are risky.

Could God have created a world with love but without human choice? Perhaps. But it would be very different than what we have now. When my wife and I brought our kids into the world, we did so at great risk. The first time I looked into the eyes of our oldest child, the thought never crossed my mind that one day, this precious baby could choose to hate me, hurt me, or reject me.

This is part of the reason that pain and suffering is such an inextricable part of the Christian life.

Understanding the pain of relational brokenness is to understand a bit more of how God feels about us when we're far from Him.

How difficult is it to lose a relationship with a passing acquaintance? Not bad. How about a friend that has been close for years? How painful is a betrayal, a death, or a loss? Much worse. Now what about a close family member or a beloved spouse? Excruciating.

In this book, we haven't shied away from some of the most difficult types of pain.

Probably the most difficult pain a human can bear is the loss of a child through broken relationships or death, as Rhett Burnett and others in Moore can testify. Why? When we lose a child, we lose someone who was, at one point, a significant part of our true identity. The closer we are, the deeper the pain when a relationship is lost.

This ties directly into a theological reality of what Christ did when He went to the cross.

Scripture is plain that "Christ died for our sins according to the Scriptures, that He was buried and that He rose again on the third day according to the Scriptures..." (I Corinthians 15:3b-4)

At times, I've had skeptics ask, "Even if He is God, how is it that Jesus' death paid the price for all the sins of everyone in the world?" How is it that Jesus could suffer enough to cover all the cumulative sins of the world?

Consider that Jesus has been in Divine relationship and community with the Father and the Holy Spirit for all eternity.

At the writing of this book, my wife and I have been married for 22 years. As close as we are and as devastating as it would be to be separated from her, Jesus was *infinitely* closer to the Heavenly Father when He willingly suffered death and separation from Him.

What part of Christ's final, torturous day hurt him the most? Worse than the emotional trauma from His friends leaving? Worse than the crown of thorns placed on His head? Worse than the beating that shredded His back and nearly killed Him? What hurt Jesus worse than anything was the suffering He endured when God the Father turned away and was temporarily separated from His Son.

It was this moment when the skies turned dark and Christ cried out with a loud voice, "My God! My God! Why have you forsaken me?!" (Matt. 27:46) This was when God the Father took all the cumulative sins of the world and placed them on Christ Jesus.

The relationship between Christ Jesus and His Father was severed temporarily in a way that we cannot fully comprehend. Since they had been together for all eternity, it was *infinitely* more painful than what anyone else could experience. Jesus suffered more in that instant than the combined suffering of mankind throughout all human history.

Relationship is why Jesus came, so that we could be in relationship with Him. Why is relational pain so excruciating for us? Because we were made in the image of God. We were made to feel and relate to others.

My dear brothers and sisters, God cares deeply about your broken relationships. He also knows exactly how you feel as you experience them.

As you walk through life mourning the loss of a relationship or struggling to put it back together, remember: He's already been there. He's there now, standing with you, crying with you, praying for you, and cheering you on.

Working on our relationships is one of the primary ways the Lord grows us up into maturity.

You can get through this.

Press in and seek Him!

It is worth it.

To hear more about Jason Head's story use the QR code below or go to www.WhereWasGod.com/book.

4

STORMS AND NATURAL DISASTERS

ARE ACTS OF GOD REALLY ACTS OF GOD?

"Now the serpent was more crafty than any of the wild animals the Lord God had made. He said to the woman, "Did God really say, 'You must not eat from any tree in the garden'?" The woman said to the serpent, "We may eat fruit from the trees in the garden, but God did say, 'You must not eat fruit from the tree that is in the middle of the garden, and you must not touch

it, or you will die.'" "You will not certainly die," the serpent said to the woman. "For God knows that when you eat from it your eyes will be opened, and you will be like God, knowing good and evil."When the woman saw that the fruit of the tree was good for food and pleasing to the eye, and also desirable for gaining wisdom, she took some and ate it. She also gave some to her husband, who was with her, and he ate it. Then the eyes of both of them were opened, and they realized they were naked; so they sewed fig leaves together and made coverings for themselves.

- Genesis 3:1-7 -

Chaplain Bunny Yekzamen will never forget the cries of anguish as she walked into the lobby. Scott and Stacey McCabe had just found out that their precious son Nicolas, age 8, had not made it out of Plaza Towers Elementary.

Scott was stunned, and he just kept repeating, "He was my only son...he was my only son..."

Bunny put her arms around Stacey and whispered to her, "I am here to walk with you through this." Through tear-filled eyes, Stacey responded, "I'm not walking right now. I'm crawling."

I believe the next moment was inspired by God himself. Bunny dropped tearfully to her knees and said, "Then I'll just crawl with you." They sobbed in each other's arms.

Now they are great friends. Bunny and the McCabes have crawled, prayed, and cried together for many months.

Bunny came to Moore as part of the Baptist Disaster Relief Chaplaincy to do what she does for all grieving people, regardless of their faith; she comforts them, cares for them emotionally and physically, and reassures them of God's unfathomable love. Bunny has served along with thousands of other volunteers on feeding units, chainsaw crews, and assessment teams after ice storms, floods, and tornadoes in several states.

She believes that God has called us to be the hands and feet of Jesus, and she lives her life in a way that convinces me and everyone else around her that she means it.

The chaplain, a mother of four grown children and devoted wife of a Muslim convert to Christianity, says she does several things to help comfort grieving people. She listens to the grieving more than she talks, fetches a cold bottle of water, searches through the rubble with them, or gives them a warm blanket, a hot cup of coffee, or a shoulder to cry on. Bunny says that her interaction with people in tragedy may last only a few moments or she may stay connected for many years.

I'm so thankful for disaster relief workers like Bunny. After living through a local community tragedy, it would be hard to overstate the value of volunteers that come in from all over the world to offer support. Fellow local pastor Don Brewer said it this way, "It's as if God called a conference for compassionate Christians and decided to convene right here in Moore."

The community is impacted by these volunteers in more ways than the obvious feeding and clean up. After a disaster, it's not just homes that are damaged and streets that need to be cleaned. The type of recovery that seems to take the longest is the emotional and spiritual recovery.

What does a natural disaster do to someone's faith? How does tragedy impact our emotional health?

Even long-time Christians deal with confusion over the apparent dichotomy in the God they believe in—that God holds the power over nature, but He is also good and loving. So, why does He allow tragedy?

Our minds and hearts are left to muddle in the unanswered questions and raw grief.

"Believers are struggling with God, who they have believed loves them and would protect them, yet He allowed it to happen," explains Bunny. "They don't want to be angry at God, but they are. They are broken, and they need help."

DURING TRAGEDY, WHAT ARE THE COMMON QUESTIONS PEOPLE ARE ASKING?

For many people, especially those who have lost children, friends, neighbors, or relatives, the question is this: *Where was God?* Where was He when the tornado ripped doors off their hinges, and slaughtered at least a hundred horses at an equine training center? Where was He when the storm scattered chunks of plaster over victims trying to find shelter in closets, in storm cellars, and in passing cars?

Where was God? And who can we blame for the calamity that with apparent callousness destroyed property, homes, hopes, and lives?

It's noteworthy, that most suffering on earth is due to the sinfulness of man. Since we are free to choose or reject God, we're also free to hurt others with our choices. From starvation in countries with unjust oppression to murderers who batter and kill in the darkness, much of our human suffering is a direct result of the free will decisions of evil people.

But these next two chapters are a more difficult topic for me to consider – what are we to make of natural disasters that wreck cities and kill children? Here, we'll deal with a series of questions that I think reflect some of the toughest philosophical and theological questions we face.

- Acts of nature are also called "acts of God." Does God cause them? Why?
- If God exists and He's all-powerful, then why doesn't He stop them?
- What are we to make of the seemingly senseless suffering and death of young innocent children?

Before I go further in this book, I want to share genuinely that I have personally spent many tear-filled and thought-filled sessions meditating on these questions. After all the books read, and time spent thinking and praying, I still don't feel qualified to present myself as an expert on these questions. I do believe that I'm gifted in loving people through hard times as a pastor. But I'm not sure we can satisfy ourselves with this great "problem of pain and suffering." I am convinced, however, that it's essential for our spiritual development to wrestle with these questions and at least try to understand some of the basic principles involved in the philosophical question, "Why does God allow pain and suffering, when it is within His power to stop it?"

Another open disclaimer I'm compelled to share is that even if I felt myself capable of explaining these difficult topics completely, I don't think my answers would give comfort to those hurting. I also don't believe that we can assign purpose to specific instances of suffering with certainty. *It's unlikely in this lifetime that we'll ever know the specific reason God allowed a specific tragedy.*

Nevertheless, we'll work to examine in this chapter what role God plays in disaster, what role we ourselves play, and what role Satan, the known enemy of our soul plays.

If we understand the part each of us plays in suffering, will that bring comfort to our hearts?

WILL FINDING SOMEONE OR SOMETHING TO BLAME HELP ME FEEL BETTER?

While having an appropriate "culprit" in mind won't heal the hurting or raise the dead, it's natural for us to quickly make mental connections that place blame. [18] We ask questions that result in the ultimate blame game. Eventually, we end up even blaming God himself as we ask the questions, sometimes angrily, sometimes sheepishly, but always in pain. "Why, God, did this happen? Why now? Why this? Why here? Why me?" We're looking for reasons to see who is at fault.

If we find something or someone to blame, will we find comfort for our hearts? I don't think so.

Dr. Brené Brown is a research professor at the University of Houston. Brown has spent a lifetime studying authentic leadership, vulnerability, shame, fear, and blame. According to her research, "blame is simply the discharging of discomfort and pain."

When we experience loss, our hearts ache. Even the most rational and logical answer would likely not satisfy our longings.

My prayer for you, my dear reader, is that you'll learn the following truth in this chapter:

WHEN I CAN'T UNDERSTAND GOD'S REASONS, I CAN ALWAYS TRUST HIS GOODNESS.

18 See the short video "Brene Brown on Blame" (https://www.YouTube.com/watch?v=RZW-f2_2L2v8, accessed July 18, 2015).

There are some stories and verses that hint at answers to our most difficult questions. We don't get the full answer, but we can get shadows of understanding. Some of this may not be what most people would expect a pastor to say when it comes to suffering and natural disasters. But here are some truths that can help us navigate our faith through the stormy waters of natural disaster and tragedy.

It all started in a garden.

HERE'S THE STORY —MAN'S FALL AND GOD'S REDEMPTIVE PLAN

What part does man play in the fact that our world is broken?

Is it possible that mankind and more specifically, you and I, hold some responsibility for the fact that our world has tsunamis, typhoons, earthquakes, and famine? Such an assertion seems counter-intuitive. We even call these tragedies "acts of God" although we might be apt to call them "acts of Satan." They seem to be out of our hands. After all, there's no way anyone would choose these things!

But, there's more to the story.

In a way, humanity *did* choose tornadoes and famine, snow and hail, and every other natural disaster and occurrence of suffering.

Come with me back in history, to the beginning of time, to a garden called Eden, which God had created for humanity to thrive, and to walk day after day in perfect fellowship with God. There were no thorns then, no Ebola, no corn blight, no snowstorms or storms of any kind. The book of Genesis records, fascinatingly, that the garden was "watered by a mist," or "streams that came up out of the ground" (Genesis 2:6) and filled with all kinds of beautiful fruits, trees, plants, and animals, none of which were afraid of humans.

At that time, no one, either animal or human, ate meat. Hunting and killing prey for food involved death, which had not yet been introduced to the world. God gave Adam and Eve "every green plant" to eat, and without the diseases that commonly attack crops today or crab grass. We can only imagine the bounty that awaited them in their lush tropical paradise: buttery macadamia nuts, tart passion fruits spilling with juice, fragrant basil leaves, nutty rice and grains. And probably a host of exotic fruits and vegetables we can't possibly imagine today.

God created it this way, for eternity.

No floods. No ice storms. No lightning strikes. No famine. Perfect growing conditions. Eating from the earth, and working the soil daily into magnificent harvests of bounty.

Until… Genesis 3. Here's where we find the story commonly called "The Fall of Man" in all of its tragedy:

> "Now the serpent was more crafty than any of the wild animals the Lord God had made. He said to the woman, "Did God really say, 'You must not eat from any tree in the garden'?"
>
> The woman said to the serpent, "We may eat fruit from the trees in the garden, but God did say, 'You must not eat fruit from the tree that is in the middle of the garden, and you must not touch it, or you will die.'"
>
> "You will not certainly die," the serpent said to the woman. "For God knows that when you eat from it your eyes will be opened, and you will be like God, knowing good and evil."

> When the woman saw that the fruit of the tree was good for food and pleasing to the eye, and also desirable for gaining wisdom, she took some and ate it. She also gave some to her husband, who was with her, and he ate it. Then the eyes of both of them were opened, and they realized they were naked; so they sewed fig leaves together and made coverings for themselves (Genesis 3:1-7).

In Scripture, Satan is referred to as either a "serpent" or a "dragon," explicitly in verses like Revelation 12:9, and in this gloomy chapter of Genesis, Satan does what we already know he enjoys: lying, (John 8:44 calls him the "father," or originator, of lies), tempting, deceiving (Revelation 12:9), and crushing them with suffering. Since Adam and Eve ultimately died because they listened to Satan's false teachings, the "serpent" deserves his label as "murderer" (John 8:44 again).

However, as easy as it might be to let humanity off the hook—after all, Satan deliberately deceived them, right? Eve, and ultimately Adam, chose to ignore God's clear instructions not to eat fruit from the Tree of Knowledge of Good and Evil. In Romans 5:12-19 we learn that their actions were categorically *sinful*.

The first sin was orchestrated by Satan, and acted out by humanity in the most beautiful garden on earth, right under God's nose.

When reflecting on this event, the Fall of Man, the worst tragedy throughout history, Oxford professor Dr. John Lennox compares it to the famous St. Michael's Cathedral (Coventry). It was destroyed in WWII bombings and still stands in ruins today. He explains, "Our world at all of its levels shows that sort of thing you see when you go to Coventry Cathedral in England. You see the traces of a past beauty, but you see that a bomb has hit it. And there is a sense that a bomb has hit our planet, because from the Biblical perspective, the rebellion of human beings against God has had effects on the planet."[19]

Indeed, our planet and our species have been hit by a cosmic bomb.

That first sin was so grotesque that it literally changed everything in an instant. Not only was there instantaneous change, but the world was set on a course of an ever worsening trajectory. Suddenly, Adam and Eve became mortals who would age, expire, and die. Thorns sprang up in the once fertile ground, and Adam would be forced to "toil" with sweat for the rest of his life rather than to enjoy hearty work. Childbearing, presumably, would have been painless and wholly joyful, but suddenly it became a thing of extreme pain: the prolonged physical agony of childbirth (oftentimes leading to death), the gaping grief of miscarriage, stillbirth, or early death of a child, and even the severing pain of letting go of grown or wayward children that tears into a tender mother's heart.

Nothing would ever be the same.

It all started with a forceful eviction from the garden. Then, enter death, not only for humans, but also for animals, plants, and creation itself. Enter suffering of hunted and slaughtered animals now needed for meat and clothing rather than companionship. Enter chaos and disorder, of offspring at war with one another. Enter murder, of Adam and Eve's first innocent son by his own brother. Enter isolation and punishment, while Cain wanders the earth, marked by God so that no one will kill him as he killed his brother.

Enter the days of men so evil that God wanted to destroy them all, and He saved only righteous Noah and his family before deluging the earth in a flood.

---

19 "The Loud Absence: Where is God in Suffering?", John Lennox and Margaret Battin, recorded lecture hosted by The Veritas Forum at the University of Utah 2013, published on YouTube February 8, 2014 (https://www.YouTube.com/watch?v=g0mcdgPDC9k, at minute mark 1:24-1:26, accessed July 18, 2015).

Enter the first recorded natural disaster: heavy rain (Genesis 2:5-6 is clear that the earth hadn't previously seen this on the earth) and unprecedented and unequalled flooding that covered the whole earth.

Who caused the fall of man? Who caused the subsequent flooding of the earth?

It started with Adam and Eve, but we all share in the guilt.

"But I'm not Adam!" you might think. "I'm not Eve! I didn't eat the fruit. So why should I, as a mere participant in humanity, be condemned along with Adam and Eve?"

Take a look at Romans 3:11-12, and 23:

> "There is no one righteous, not even one;
> there is no one who understands;
> there is no one who seeks God.
> All have turned away,
> they have together become worthless;
> there is no one who does good,
> not even one...
> ***for all have sinned and fall short of the glory of God...***"

There we have it: One of the many, many Scriptures that show us clearly that we, on an individual, personal level, are also at fault in this whole debacle.

We are sinners, with our initial sinless nature broken both because we inherited it from Adam and Eve, our ancestors. We're also sinners by our own choice when we regularly choose to go against what we know is right.

We all share directly in the fall of man and the broken world we live in. In fact, based on what we know about Adam and Eve, about our own natures, about God's sovereignty and His foreknowledge of what He knows we are capable of, I'm convinced that if ***I myself had been there in place of Adam, I would have done the exact same thing.***

We are the ones who choose daily to live in sin. We have all, individually and collectively, participated in the destruction of God's creation, which was made to be perfect and without suffering, and we are all responsible, in part, for every natural disaster that has ever come from a world that's now stunted with sin, death, and suffering (Romans 8:18-25).

At this point, we can't turn back to Eden. *Eden is gone.* Nothing will make this world kinder and gentler until God creates the new heaven and the new earth, as predicted in Revelation 21:1 and Romans 8:18-25.

Now the world aches with brokenness, pain, and sin. We yearn to undo the memories and the knowledge of tragedy. The nightmarish images that stick in our heads even years later stay here to haunt us, bringing with them even more sinister crimes that test the limits of human comprehension: animal torture, child abuse, mass genocide, and many forms of cruelty too tragic to mention here.

We got what we wanted in the beginning, not just the Knowledge of Good, but the Knowledge of Evil.

At this point some of us might want to throw up our hands and blame God for allowing us to set off an inexorable path to destruction started by one tiny cog (Adam and Eve, the tree in the garden), but we'd be missing something. Something big and weighty. Something so huge that it changes everything.

Skip ahead from the doom of Genesis 3 to the end of the chapter, where God lovingly clothes Adam and Eve with skins (i.e. flesh of a slaughtered animal, which constitutes the first death), and see the tender mercy of God, even toward sinners.

Since Adam and Eve had obviously never known butchery, or killing, or the concept of leather or wool coming from animal flesh, they tried—insufficiently—to rely on fig leaves and plants, the way they'd always done in Eden. Except this time it didn't work. And it never would work again. Leaves would no longer be sufficient for the cold and the elements, and only blood spilled in sacrifice of a sheep, of the Lamb of God, could take away their nakedness and shame.

A picture of the cross and redemption, right there in the garden, in the face of sin. A flicker, a shimmer, a hint of the promised Messiah in humanity's darkest hour. A promise that there was yet hope!

This incredible destruction in the Garden of Eden launched the rule of Satan here on Earth. But even this would be temporary.

In Genesis 3:15, we catch even more of the hope to come. Satan's head would one day be crushed, symbolizing the end of his rule on this earth and breaking the bondage that was created in the Garden. But the demolition of the enemy would come at a great price. This price would be the suffering and brokenness of One who would be born of a woman. This prophecy pointed clearly to the day that Jesus Christ, God's Son, would be sent to Earth to live the perfect life. To then be falsely accused and tortured, hung on a cross, and buried, forever paying the price for our sins, for our brokenness.

It was love that did it. It was love that caused our heavenly Father to send Jesus, His only begotten Son to suffer and bleed and die. It was the love of our Father that gave us a promise of redemption even at the worst point in human history.

But wait! There's more. Look at the last verses that close out the chapter:

> And the Lord God said, "The man has now become like one of us, knowing good and evil. He must not be allowed to reach out his hand and take also from the tree of life

> and eat, and live forever." So the Lord God banished him from the Garden of Eden to work the ground from which he had been taken. After he drove the man out, he placed on the east side of the Garden of Eden cherubim and a flaming sword flashing back and forth to guard the way to the tree of life."

In reference to the shocked and crushed couple (whom He'd already tenderly clothed), God says, "He must not be allowed to reach out his hand and take also from the tree of life and eat, and live forever."

But even after removing them from the garden, God still tenderly loved and cared for His creation.

God didn't leave Adam and Eve to freeze to death; he clothed them. They learned how to grow enough food to survive, and then they went on to love, to have children, to pass hundreds of years together, and to create a family that would become the basis of all civilization. Abel raised livestock, and Cain farmed. Cain's descendants lived in tents, forged tools of bronze and iron, and discovered the joys of musical instruments.

While typing this now, I'm thinking about a few of the great things in life. We were meant to embrace the beauty around us. The music that soothes. The red velvet cake I just ate that pleased my palate and broke my diet all at once. The beauty outside with the wind, sun, and grass. The joy in my kid's laughter from the next room. The beautiful friendship and love my wife and I share. God gives us joys and comforts, even in this fallen world.

Eve ultimately credited God with granting her children, a sign of her burgeoning faith, and after the horrors of Abel's murder and Cain's banishment God gave them baby Seth to comfort them in their loss.

Seth raised Enosh, and in Enosh's day, "men began to call on the name of the Lord" (Genesis 4:26).

Just as we do today.

In the hardest of times, God still gives grace. And He's still there waiting for us when we turn to Him.

Because of God's mercy, we can look forward to eternity with *perfection*, with the absence of sin: a restored Eden, snatched from the teeth of the serpent by Jesus, the Lion of Judah. Then and only then, with our sinful souls washed clean by the blood of the Lamb and his atoning sacrifice, will we be able to enjoy sinless, soul-quenching paradise with no aging, sickness, or pain.

We will walk with our Lord as Adam and Eve did, in the cool of the day, only this time it will be forever.

With this view of God's incredible mercy and love, it almost makes us wonder, "Why on earth is it so hard to trust Him?"

The story of all time and history, the greatest love story in existence, is the story of creation, the fall of man, then God's pursuit to restore us to relationship with Him. In the end, everything will be put back together, making things right again.

But in the meantime, everything is broken. Our world is broken, which causes natural disasters, hardships, death, and dying. Also, our hearts and our relationships with our Creator are broken.

Every single disaster and tragedy we see has been directly caused by the tragedy from the Garden of Eden.

But that's not all. Not only is our universe broken and damaged, we also have an Enemy who is responsible for causing many of the tragedies we see in our world.

HERE'S THE ENEMY — ACTIVELY SEEKING TO DESTROY YOUR FAITH

The Bible depicts Satan as the enemy of God (and therefore also the enemy of God's people) is also the creator of darkness, of wickedness, and of every evil thing.

Scripture consistently underscores this truth in passage after passage, like this one from 1 Peter 5:8: "Be alert and of sober mind. Your enemy the devil prowls around like a roaring lion looking for someone to devour."

If you've ever seen a lion devour something like a hapless gazelle, it isn't pretty. It's calculated, gory, and gruesome. That's how Satan waits for us, ready to pounce at every moment, licking his bloody jaws.

The book of Job clearly states that Satan requested to inflict pain on righteous Job, and once God granted him permission, Satan went out and struck him with disease, the sudden death of his ten children, painful boils, and a whole host of unimaginable physical and emotional blows, one right after the other. Like a punch in the gut, Satan seems almost gleeful at the opportunity to harm Job.

Take a look at the beginning:

> One day the angels came to present themselves before the Lord, and Satan also came with them. The Lord said to Satan, "Where have you come from?"
>
> Satan answered the Lord, "From roaming throughout the earth, going back and forth on it."
>
> Then the Lord said to Satan, "Have you considered my servant Job? There is no one on earth like him; he is blameless and upright, a man who fears God and shuns

> evil."
>
> "Does Job fear God for nothing?" Satan replied. "Have you not put a hedge around him and his household and everything he has? You have blessed the work of his hands, so that his flocks and herds are spread throughout the land. But now stretch out your hand and strike everything he has, and he will surely curse you to your face."
>
> The Lord said to Satan, "Very well, then, everything he has is in your power, but on the man himself do not lay a finger."
>
> Then Satan went out from the presence of the Lord" (Job 1:6-12).

It's obvious that Satan "went out" from God's presence to destroy Job, as far as God's limits would allow. Based on Satan's exuberant willingness to afflict Job, had God not given any parameters, there's no telling what Satan might have done.

Why does the Bible say that Satan roams? Because unlike our Heavenly Father, Satan is not all-present; he cannot be more than one place at a time. Many would like to make Satan out to be the dark side to God's dual nature, but such a thing is quite opposed to the clear teaching of scripture.

God, as the transcendent Creator, is above all. Satan, the enemy of our souls is a created being. Initially, he was one of God's angels whose heart was filled with pride. He fell from Heaven, taking a third of the angels with him. After Satan's attempt to overthrow the Lord and "make myself like the Most High," God has allowed him to roam about the Earth for a limited time (Revelation 12:7-12).

Consider the diametric opposite of God's good nature and character as revealed in 2 Chronicles 16:9: "For the eyes of the Lord range throughout the earth to strengthen those whose hearts are fully committed to him."

In fact, almost every single instance of Satan in the Bible comes with an association to evil or suffering. Satan is the one in Luke 22:31 who would "sift Peter as wheat," and he's the one who specifically kept a "daughter of Abraham" painfully hunched over and "bound" for eighteen agonizing years before Jesus healed her body and set her free (Luke 13:11.)

It was Satan who directly caused not one but two natural disasters to afflict Job: fire from Heaven, and a strong wind that collapsed the house where Job's grown children were feasting.

God offered parameters to "test" Job (and blessed Job mightily after he was found faithful) but the clear perpetrator of the acts themselves was none other than Satan.

Satan is the one who laughs as typhoon waves slam into the Japanese coast, taking souls with it. He rubs his hands with delight as he dries up the clouds so that people faint from drought.

Satan—not God—is the one who delights in evil, suffering, and destruction. Were it not for God's intervention and gracious parameters, who knows how much of the earth would be left?

It's easy for us as followers of Christ to attribute causative blame to Satan. But we need to also understand that it's not only Satan that causes natural disasters.

It's important to note that God alone is Sovereign over nature. Satan can only wreak as much havoc as God Himself allows. Just in the case of Job, God could very well stop any given tragedy from happening.

We can't know the extent that Satan is involved in any particular tragedy in the same way that we can't know what God's ultimate purpose is for allowing bad things to happen. Is this particular tragedy due to the laws of nature running their course? Is this storm part of a demonic plan to hurt the people in its path? Or does God have some other reason for it?

So now we'll address another question that niggles in the back of our minds, even with such a beautiful—and wholly true—picture of our merciful God. There's another angle of natural disasters that we've yet to uncover if we want to see the whole, undiluted picture of God and who He is.

In my broken humanity, I would like to sum this entire chapter up now by saying, "So there you have it. The responsibility is all on the devil and sinful people for the broken world we live in." I'd really like to say, "God Himself, you see, doesn't 'cause' natural disasters. He simply 'allows' them."

Right...?

This next section is the one that's hardest for most people to swallow.

HERE'S OUR LORD — SOVEREIGN OVER ALL NATURE![20]

In July of 2013, just two months after the May devastation in our community, one of the largest natural disasters in our state's history, we contacted 40,000 homes, all in the tornado affected zip

20 Some of the thoughts in this section were suggested by the blog article, "God and Natural Disasters" by Erwin W. Lutzer at moodymedia.org, 2005 (http://www.moodymedia.org/articles/god-and-natural-disasters/, accessed July 18, 2015).

codes, and directed them to an online survey. We wanted to know the community's most common spiritual questions. The survey was simple. A few questions would verify they were in our target area. Then the big question:

"If you could ask God anything and you knew He would answer, what would you ask?"

There were hundreds of responses. A few were attacks on the church or on God Himself. Some asked specific questions for guidance. Some were questions about difficult Bible passages. All were poignant.

After painstakingly compiling the data, here's what we found:

The top question understandably had to do with our shared tragic day of May 20, 2013. The respondents wanted to know, "Why did God allow the EF5 tornado to shred our town, our homes, our school, and our children? Where was God?" The next most common question was similar, but more general. "Why does God allow suffering?" The third most popular question was, "Why does God allow evil?"

All three questions combined meant that over 60% of respondents asked a question about the existence of pain and suffering. As I've repeated throughout this book, I'm convinced this question is the single most difficult question to tackle as a Christian.

Some aspects of the question of pain are easier to grasp than others.

Take the question of why evil exists, for instance. Think about the evil perpetrated by Stalin, Hitler, Chairman Mau, Osama Bin Laden, or in more recent days, by the terrorist group ISIS. Why would God allow those who are so clearly evil to perpetrate their sinister actions on others? Why does He allow them to exist at all?

We live in a world with love and moral choice. In God's sovereign pleasure, He created us to love Him. But to love is to have a choice. We aren't simply programmed like machines to accept or reject Him. We have the capacity to say "yes" or "no" to His love as well as we could reject the love of anyone else. A common way to explain this is to use our kids as an example.

I remember well the birth of my first child, Alyssa. Looking into her tiny face, holding her tender hand, I was aware that even though her mother and I brought her into this world, as she grows, she could one day chose to hate me. As painful as that would be, such is the reality of living in a world where love and choice exist.

Additionally, within each of us is the capacity for great evil. If God decided to eliminate all evil from the world today, how many of us would still be here tomorrow? Or, as Dr. John Lennox, professor of Mathematics at Oxford and Christian apologist says, "To wish for a world without evil is to wish myself out of existence."[21]

It's also easy enough to grasp the notion of a great Evil One that is the Enemy of our souls. This story is something nearly innate to us. Good and evil. Heroes and villains. Good guys and bad guys. So the reality of Satan "causing" a disastrous ruckus here on Earth in an attempt to destroy us is something that we can accept.

But again we ask, what are we to make of natural disasters? How do we process emotionally and spiritually the fact that there is a Sovereign God that exists, who is all powerful, who could step in at any time to prevent disaster and still sometimes simply does not?

Inspired by the great minds of C. S. Lewis and Professor Lennox, I ask these questions: Could God have created a world with storms

---

21 "The Loud Absence: Where is God in Suffering?", John Lennox and Margaret Battin, recorded lecture hosted by The Veritas Forum at the University of Utah 2013, published on YouTube February 8, 2014 (https://www.YouTube.com/watch?v=g0mcdgPDC9k, at minute mark 1:24-1:26, accessed July 18, 2015).

that water the earth but don't ever flood it? Could He have designed lightening to fill the soil as it does with nitrogen, but in a way that the lightening wouldn't hurt a person? Could we have fire that warms our hands, but won't burn when we get too close? Obviously God has the power to create whatever He pleases, as well as the intelligence and moral superiority to create greater natural objects and forces than we can fathom. So why didn't He?

We simply can't answer these questions adequately enough to satisfy our gnawing grief.

There is no palatable way to explain the reasons behind God's involvement (or apparent non-involvement, from our perspective) in natural disasters, or why He allows destruction that He obviously has the power to stop. There are no simple answers. I'm convinced the only solution is to work to understand God's sovereignty better, and His goodness. ***And when we can't understand God's reasons, we trust in His nature.***

How is it that God is both all powerful and good simultaneously, given the broken world we live in? I don't know, but I can testify that He is. My prayer is that as we reflect, we can gain wisdom because in the words of German Old Testament scholar Gerhard von Rad, "Wisdom is an awareness of a complex reality."[22]

What do we, as finite human beings, know about the nature of a holy, powerful, and eternal God?

During natural disasters, is God removed from the picture altogether? Does He stand back and watch, like a spectator at a soccer game? Does He set the earth up according to certain natural standards and then refuse to participate while it "does its thing?"

---

22 Cited in "Walking With God through Pain and Suffering" by Timothy Keller (New York: Penguin Group, 2013), 138.

These questions have ached in the hearts of men for centuries. Strangely enough, the Bible has a clear answer to where God was during the Moore tornado and every other natural disaster that has struck the earth since the fall of Eden.

He was there.

Furthermore, we already know from encounters with Satan in the book of Job (and hundreds of other examples in Scripture) that God is sovereign over nature, over the wind, and the seas. He is even sovereign and in full control over natural disasters.

Dr. Sam Storms, a local Oklahoma City pastor and council member for The Gospel Coalition, posted an article addressing this on the very day of the Moore tornado. In his article, "Tornadoes, Tsunamis, and the Mystery of Suffering and Sovereignty," Storms says

> ***God is absolutely sovereign over all of nature.*** He can Himself send devastation. Or He may permit Satan to wreak havoc in the earth. Yes he can, if he chooses, intervene and prevent a tornado, a tsunami, and all other natural disasters. In the end, we do not know why he makes one choice and not another. In the end, we like Job, must join the apostle Paul and say: "Oh, the depth of the riches and wisdom and knowledge of God! ***How unsearchable are his judgments and how inscrutable are his ways!*** For who has known the mind of the Lord, or who has been his counselor? Or who has given a gift to him that he might be repaid? For from him and through him and to him are all things. To him be glory forever. Amen."[23]

---

23 "Tornadoes, Tsunamis, and the Mystery of Suffering and Sovereignty" in Enjoying God at samstorms.com, May 20, 2013 (http://www.samstorms.com/enjoying-god-blog/post/tornadoes--tsunamis--and-the-mystery-of-suffering-and-sovereignty, accessed July 18, 2015). Emphases are original.

In other words, God has the power to stop every natural disaster.

But sometimes He doesn't.

It may not feel "right" or even holy to suggest God is responsible in the face of disaster, but the Bible does not shrink away from the fact that *God is sovereignly responsible*. He has the power to tell the winds to die down, and the waters to recede (or to fall, when it is desperately needed), and yet many times He refrains.

This seems to fly right in the face of everything we've heard about God being loving and compassionate, doesn't it? At first glance, maybe it appears that way. But there's more to the story if we dig a bit deeper.

Before we go further, I'd like to deal with a comment we hear from Christians at this point in the discussion. Commonly, I hear people say that God doesn't really "cause" such disasters—He passively "allows" them through the natural means he established at creation.

This is many times heard especially after someone experiences a tragic loss. A pat on the shoulder, and, "Just remember, God doesn't cause these things. He allows them, but He doesn't cause them."

Certainly, by his Divine privilege, God does "allow" events to happen, by giving them permission to occur, as is clearly stated in the book of Job. God gave permission to Satan to send trouble on Job, but only at His parameters, and by His specifications. In fact, Scripture tells us God releases and binds Satan at will, and He alone gives natural laws and events their limits.

Satan does cause the evil that befalls this earth. We do live in a fallen, sinful, post-Edenic world, which groans from the pain of humanity and brokenness and longs for redemption. Those are all true.

But if by "allow" we mean that God is not still in control over nature and these tragic events, or if we mean that He stands back and watches events unfold without some level of involvement, I think we misunderstand what sovereignty means.

Telling grieving people that God just "allows" tragic things, might be more comfortable for us. We hope that they won't blame God and turn away from Him, but it's important for us not to discount the fact that God is still sovereign. He is still in control. He could have stopped this tragedy, but He didn't. We don't know the reason He didn't prevent this particular tragedy, but He is still God, He is still good, and we can still trust Him.

Remember: ***Trusting and following God doesn't mean never having doubts or questions. It just means to keep trusting Him even though I still have questions.***

The sovereignty of God is a blessed truth that we should feverishly cling to. If God isn't sovereign over all, then indeed, we have no hope. No hope, no Christ, no deliverance, and no eternity.

All of suffering and pain was initially introduced to the world by mankind who chose to rebel against God and caused a cosmic explosion.

Much of our suffering and pain is caused by Satan as he works to destroy our faith.

But God is still completely in control and sovereign over all. Is God worthy of my trust even when I don't understand his purpose for allowing disaster? Yes. I can trust Him even with my most pointed, difficult, and direct questions.

In the next chapter, we'll continue to discuss natural disasters, but rather than looking at the causes for them, we'll instead try to reflect on the question, "How can I find God in this tragedy?" I'm confident that as you walk through a struggle, you'll find the next chapter to be very meaningful.

To hear more about faith in the face of natural disasters use the QR code below or go to www.WhereWasGod.com/book.

5

STORMS AND NATURAL DISASTERS – CONTINUED

FINDING GOD IN TRAGEDY

For he spoke and stirred up a tempest
that lifted high the waves.
They mounted up to the heavens and went down to the depths;
in their peril their courage melted away.

They reeled and staggered like drunkards;
they were at their wits' end.
Then they cried out to the LORD *in their trouble,*
and he brought them out of their distress.
He stilled the storm to a whisper;
the waves of the sea were hushed.
They were glad when it grew calm,
and he guided them to their desired haven.

- Psalm 107:25-30 -

Amy Simpson, then the principal of Plaza Towers Elementary School in Moore, was huddled in the bathroom with several other staff members when the building literally collapsed around them.

"There goes the roof," recalls Amy, also mother of two and native of Moore. "I looked up and that's when I could see the sky and debris... I saw things floating by. It was like slow motion."

When she finally was able to push open the bathroom door, she was relieved to find the wall still standing. So she turned the corner and nearly walked into the bumper of a car. She remembers, "There's a car in the office. It's on top of the desk."

As Amy crawled over piles of debris from the ruined school building, she immediately began to see evidence of the Divine. She had a surreal sense of calm throughout the whole ordeal, and help poured in from the neighborhood as soon as the storm passed.

"I believe that God was there because of the peace I had and that He allowed my mom and my husband to get through on the phone. After that moment, lots of people came in from everywhere. They must have just been sitting there waiting for the storm to pass so they could come and help us. Some with shoes, some without. They already had bolt cutters, shovels, and everything they needed to help us. They had gloves already, too."

Amy, a Christian believer since her youth, says she has no doubts about God's presence even in the worst of the storm.

"There's no other explanation. As far as God's grace and His peace that day, when I think back I didn't recognize it when I was in the bathroom. I didn't recognize it when I was telling those parents, 'Get your kids! They're down here. Go get them. Be calm! Don't scare my other kids.' Looking back there's no reason I should have been the one saying, 'It's okay. We're going to get through this. Go calmly.' I couldn't have been calm by myself. I know myself," Amy says. "I don't get riled up about everything, but I also know that I can get scared and I can be afraid. I can be nervous and anxious and I can get mad, and all of those emotions would have been okay that day, had I felt them. But God didn't allow me to go those places. He allowed me to be in His embrace. I never once thought I was going to die. That scares me now. I certainly am not immortal, but it scares me now that I wasn't scared then. But there's only one explanation. It had to be God."

Amy, whose two children and firefighter husband also survived the tornado, says she has been different since that day. And what the educators communicate to the children they teach has changed, too.

"The teachers here are so resilient," she says. "So many of them came back when it would have been a lot easier to take a year off. After such a traumatic ordeal, it would have been easier for them to say, 'I want to go somewhere else.' But they've been here for the kids. So for us, teaching is a lot more than just books, ABCs, and 123s. We're teaching our kids that it's okay to be scared, it's okay to be brave, it's okay to take a chance. I believe that's how those kids felt at the beginning of the school year following the tornado: 'I'm taking a chance going to school now. I may not be safe here, but life goes on.'"

As far as what Amy has learned about God from her tornado experience, it's this: He's everywhere. "I always knew it, but I recognize it more now... while driving, if someone stops short or if I nearly miss something in the road, I immediately say, 'Thank you, Jesus.' Because He is in all these little things" she says. ***"Once you're in a horrible experience and find God's grace and peace during that, you recognize Him everywhere."***

So where is God, then, when the walls crumble, when the dam breaks, when children cry for rain and relief from the heat? If He is loving and kind and longs to reach out to humanity even through suffering, where is He? And why does He seem so far away?

God is there. He is there in the midst of the storm, healing, protecting, cradling, comforting, calling souls home, and drawing men and women to Himself. In fact, I'm convinced that we can experience His grace, peace, and presence in an even clearer way during disasters than perhaps at any other time.

Here are some steps I encourage you to consider for the next time you walk through an unexpected setback or tragedy.

1. EXPERIENCE GOD'S GRACE AND KINDNESS, ESPECIALLY IN TRAGEDY.

In the last chapter, we considered the big idea: **When I can't understand God's reasons, I can always trust His goodness.** Now in this chapter, we're going to be looking more at what God's character is, what His nature is exactly that we should be trusting in.

If we want the truth about God's nature or His thoughts, then we have to look back to Scripture, the same place in which He boldly speaks of His sovereignty in calamity.

And what do we find?

Page after page, book after book, we discover that the same God who claims sovereignty over disaster also insists that He is loving, kind, longsuffering, compassionate, slow to anger, quick to forgive, and tenderhearted.

It may not be natural or easy for us to use these adjectives to describe the same God who let gas clouds smother the people of Pompeii until they were buried in layers of ash, or the same God who allowed the walls of elementary schools in Moore collapse on innocent children.

But consider how the Bible describes God through the prophet Isaiah: "Can a mother forget the baby at her breast and have no compassion on the child she has borne? Though she may forget, I will not forget you! See, I have engraved you on the palms of my hands; your walls are ever before me" (Isaiah 49:15-16).

Consider Jesus, God in the flesh, who touched blind men, demon-possessed exiles, and lepers with kind hands, and gave honor to prostitutes and "sinful women" that people shunned.

"He will not quarrel or cry out; no one will hear his voice in the streets," writes Isaiah about Jesus. "A bruised reed he will not break, and a smoldering wick he will not snuff out" (Isaiah 42:2-3).

A kindhearted Jesus who "tends his flock like a shepherd: He gathers the lambs in his arms and carries them close to his heart; he gently leads those that have young" (Isaiah 40:11).

How can this be? How can we juxtapose the two images of destruction and kindness, or calamity and tender love?

Well, friends, this is where we have to leave behind our own limited assessments, if we really want to know God's heart and "lean not on our own understanding" (Proverbs 3:5-6)."

Remember what God says in Isaiah 55:8-9 about His own character:

> *My thoughts are nothing like your thoughts,' says the LORD.*
> *'And my ways are far beyond anything you could imagine.*
> *For just as the heavens are higher than the earth, so my ways are higher than your ways and my thoughts higher than your thoughts.*

In other words, whatever conclusions you might come to about the nature of God, they're not even close to the truth of who God really is. He's so much better, so much greater, so much higher than you can possibly imagine.

When Job questioned (or rather, accused) God about why He had allowed such monstrous suffering to fall upon him, a righteous man, God responded with these forceful words:

> "Who is this that obscures my plans
> with words without knowledge?
> Brace yourself like a man;
> I will question you,
> and you shall answer me" (Job 38:1-2).

The rest of the passage seems to shout with God's sovereignty over the universe—and His Divine right to it, as Creator. God's overwhelming response is so great that we get the impression that His expansive wisdom simply could not be reduced to a size small enough for Job to swallow it.

When Job asked the question, "God, where were you when this happened?" God's direct answer was to return the same question, "No

Job, the question is, where were you?" Where were you when I was out creating the stars, stocking the heavenly storehouses with snow, and helping the mountain goats give birth? Where were you, Job, if you know so much?

Exactly.

God has ways and reasons that are beyond our capacity to grasp. We can't see what the Lord is doing behind the scenes, and if we could see it, we still wouldn't understand it.

Just because I don't know what God's purpose for allowing tragedy is, that doesn't mean that there isn't a purpose for it.

Job was unaware. Unaware of God's bigger plan. Unaware of the importance of this great, intricate, narrative story that he was part of.

Just like every one of us, Job experienced life as the main character in his life story. But the story of our lives is the story of Christ, and each of us, including Job, are just supporting cast members.

We get up, we live our lives, and we shake our fists at the heavens for those aching losses and disappointments.

But how very little we know about what God is doing.

If we find that God is worthy of our trust even in the darkest circumstances, then we should accept the fact that God does have purposes for our suffering. In fact, it's likely there are thousands of purposes for each specific instance of suffering.

Anytime God allows something to happen, this creates ripple effects through the waters of time. Everything that happens impacts scores of other circumstances, and this chain of cause and effect will not stop until time is no more.

Only a sovereign God is qualified to run the universe. Only a good, gracious, and all powerful God is worthy of our trust, worship, and support as He does what only He can do.

Allowing tragedy does not mean God delights in or enjoys tragedy. It simply means He has *permitted and purposed* it to happen, according to His good will and plans. God uses disasters to strengthen our faith and mold us into His likeness. Satan is the one who uses disaster to destroy our faith and corrupt God's image within us.

As much as Satan would like to convince us that God is small-minded and vindictive like he is, Scripture breathes, whispers, shouts exactly the opposite.

God is love... God is salvation... God is a healer... God is compassionate to the broken... God is pursuer of the lost... God cares for the dying... God sees even the smallest sparrow fall... God prepares an eternal place for those who love Him, far removed from sickness or death... God will wipe every tear from our eyes...

And so we must do two things when disaster strikes, and our hearts begin to accuse the God of love. First, we must revise our narrative.

Destroy the accusations whispering through our minds like enemy propaganda: that God doesn't love us, that He doesn't care, that He's punishing us unfairly, or that He loves someone else more.

We have to fight these tempting lies as Jesus did with Scripture, with memorized and prayed-out-loud verses to remind us exactly who God is. Even if we cap our prayers with an admission of doubt ("I do believe! Help my unbelief!" Mark 9:24), the truth will still take root in us, still begin to sprout, still grow.

Quite possibly the best advice for sustaining even a fragile faith during hard times comes from Ephesians 6:10-18:

> Finally, be strong in the Lord and in his mighty power. Put on the full armor of God, so that you can take your stand against the devil's schemes. For our struggle is not

> against flesh and blood, but against the rulers, against the authorities, against the powers of this dark world and against the spiritual forces of evil in the heavenly realms. Therefore put on the full armor of God, so that when the day of evil comes, you may be able to stand your ground, and after you have done everything, to stand. Stand firm then, with the belt of truth buckled around your waist, with the breastplate of righteousness in place, and with your feet fitted with the readiness that comes from the gospel of peace. In addition to all this, take up the shield of faith, with which you can extinguish all the flaming arrows of the evil one. Take the helmet of salvation and the sword of the Spirit, which is the word of God. And pray in the Spirit on all occasions with all kinds of prayers and requests. With this in mind, be alert and always keep on praying for all the Lord's people.

This approach not only gives us weapons to use against an incorrect assessment of God's character, but it also clearly defines the real enemy: Satan. When we don't understand everything God does or doesn't do, we can come back to the truth that God loves us, that God cares deeply for us on an intimate level that we can't comprehend (Psalm 139), and that somehow He has promised to work out all things including tragedy, death, and destruction for our personal good and our spiritual growth (Romans 8:28-29). We know that death is not the end, and that He has prepared a place for us more wonderful than we can imagine, where Eden is restored, and where man and God can walk freely together, separated eternally from death and pain and suffering.

Not only should we revise our narrative and stop listening to the enemy voices telling us that God doesn't love us, but secondly, we must *trust.* When tragedy strikes and it doesn't make sense, we can either follow our limited understanding, or we can choose to *trust and have faith in the heart God claims to have.*

Trust is where the line is drawn in the sand. Faith. Trust. Belief. In spite of all perceptions that rise up to accuse the Almighty.

Faith is forged by walking in darkness and accepting what we know of God to be true.

This trust in God's nature should be a starting point for us as believers. This is the pin that holds everything together. That no matter what we think, our assumptions aren't truth. The truth is found in what God reveals about Himself. In scripture, we find a God who is infinitely more loving than we can possibly imagine.

This God, who rescued Hagar, the sobbing young mother in the desert—that's the God she called "El Roi," or "the God who sees me." This God who was compassionately willing to spare an entire wicked city on account of only ten righteous people, even though their cruelty and godlessness pained his heart. This God, who clothed Himself in flesh and walked on dusty streets, preaching and healing and teaching the lost, raising the dead, driving out demons, and breaking bread with sinners.

This God who wept over the city that would reject Him, and who prayed for forgiveness on those who pounded nails into His flesh. This is the kind of God who inspires people like Amy Simpson to rise up and become a hero in a time of need.

I encourage you to lean into His kindness, look for it, rest in it, and trust in it!

The next thing you can do to find God in the midst of natural disaster is to:

2. EMBRACE GOD'S PROVISION FOR OUR GREATEST NEEDS.

Sam Porter is the Director of Oklahoma Disaster Relief for the Baptist General Convention of Oklahoma. Sam has become a personal hero of mine as a result of meeting him through the Moore tornado disaster. He's an impressive leader and easy to follow. He's a former college football player and lives on a ranch here in Oklahoma. He communicates well with men and women alike, inspiring them to commit their lives to volunteering in the most difficult disaster zones in the world.

Listening to Sam talk about world tragedies is like getting a history lesson. He's been on site for every major world disaster over the past 20 plus years. He was even part of overseeing chaplains when the twin towers were struck by terrorists on 9/11/2001 in New York City. From earthquakes in Haiti to the tsunami in Indonesia, he has seen it all.

When you hear Sam talk about disaster relief, he is very clear about what the greatest needs of people are. It's relatively simple to bring food, water, clothing, and laborers. But the *greatest* needs in the aftermath of a disaster are spiritual and emotional.

Our friend and Disaster Relief Chaplain Bunny Yekzamen agrees.

Chaplain Bunny says those who hold fast to God and believe His promises in spite of their horrific circumstances, are amazing, courageous people.

Though they may not seem so trusting at first.

"Many people go through a stage of questioning, but not all will blame God," she says.

Questioning God isn't always a bad thing. The psalmists repeatedly questioned God even in writings that were intended for public worship. In Psalm 10:1, the Psalmist painfully asks, "Why, Lord do you stand far off? Why do you hide yourself in times of trouble?" In the following verses, we ride emotional waves with the writer until he once again expresses faith. As he closes this psalm, he writes, "The Lord is King for ever and ever; the nations will perish from his land" (Psalm 10:16).

Many psalms follow similar patterns.

Is it possible to go too far in questioning God?

I don't suggest that we should let anger at God rage without boundaries. Maturity dictates that even in our pain, we don't lash out in hurtful ways towards others. This should apply to the way we question God as well.

The book of Job is fascinating in the way it handles questioning God. Initially, in Job's grief, he professed, "... the Lord gave and the Lord has taken away; may the name of the Lord be praised" (Job 1:21). This reminds us of the laments we read in the Psalms. But beginning in Job 3 where his entire speech is a cursing of the day he was born, Job starts to allow bitterness to creep into his grief and even take root in his spirit. At this point, his harsh line of questioning **did** bring on correction from the Lord. But even when God corrected Job for his bitterness, this correction was in order to get Job back into the humble, righteous, and trusting relationship that God and Job enjoyed previously.

In our suffering, in our questioning, it is good to be honest with God about everything we're experiencing. This is part of God's closeness to us. But even in our darkest times of questioning, let's make sure that we respect who we're talking to... the Lord of all creation.

How can I know if in my deep grief, I start declining into a spiritual or emotional mindset that might damage my relationship with God or others? A Christian grief counselor might be better equipped to handle these sorts of questions. I will suggest this: if your off-and-on anger – those normal and natural human emotions involved in grief start turning into bitterness towards God, life, or other people, it's time to check your emotions and spirit, and possibly get professional help.

But no matter what, even in the darkest moments, God is there waiting for us to walk right back into His arms.

Some may question God and walk away. But some have faith that stands through even the most difficult test.

"The faith that stands the test," says Bunny, "is powerful."

"I am amazed at some of the people I have ministered to and the depth of loss they have had from a natural disaster, and even other things like cancer, a sudden accident, suicide, war, and more, and still they remained faithful," she says. "I have to tell you that the ones who stay faithful are those who truly know the Lord as their Savior, and when they do, wow! Their faith inspires and encourages me."

Inevitably, people who have experienced loss but still trust the Lord end up ministering to the very people who came to help them in their time of need.

"Their faith is so real and deep," says Bunny, "that I never see them turn away from the Lord. They hurt deeply but still remain faithful, and now they use the death of their child as an opportunity to minister to others."

This, says Bunny, is where the proverbial rubber meets the road.

For her and others like her, bringing people to God, whether through physical comfort or emotional guidance or a gentle demonstration of God's great love, is the most important thing they do.

And not surprisingly, Bunny has seen God reach out to people during natural disasters almost like a revival, showing how utterly concerned He is not only about people's hearts, but their eternal souls as well.

She recalls a visit to Texas after Hurricane Ike in a small town that had lost its power. She was serving on the feeding crew, but after days of diminishing crowds and thankless attitudes coming from people who didn't even seem to need the food, she and the crew leaders began to feel like their service was no longer useful.

"We all began to ask the question, 'Why are we still here?' Suddenly, as if the Holy Spirit spoke to each of our hearts simultaneously, we looked at each other and said, 'God isn't finished here yet,'" Bunny recalls. "'We can't see what He sees, and He knows something we don't.'"

The group prayed for forgiveness for their wrong attitudes, and the next day proceeded to prepare lunch. Bunny says a food truck full of unneeded food arrived, and after that, a couple seeking help. The group sent the food truck driver inside for lunch, and then as chaplain, Bunny stepped away from the cooking to help the couple.

Right then, says Bunny, something began to happen.

While helping gather supplies for the family, they also engaged with them in a conversation about God, Jesus, salvation, and faith. This couple decided to make Jesus the Lord of their lives. Shortly after that, the food truck delivery driver also decided to become a follower of Jesus.

"That night as we served our final meal in drive-through format, car after car began to line up. They drove through to get their food and then were able to go into another line for prayer with me, the chaplain," says Bunny. "I was blown away as car after car pulled into the prayer line and waited to be prayed with. People wanted prayer for healing for illness, of restoration of broken families, for rededication of their lives to Christ. One man got out of his car and fell onto his knees praying for forgiveness and salvation."

That day, according to Bunny, is why they were there.

Not only did the poor children of the community have a chance to eat three full meals a day (which local teachers said ordinarily didn't happen), but God had poured out a small revival on the town in response to their brokenness and the crew's openness to serve. God was meeting the deepest needs in the hearts and minds of this community.

No matter how deep the loss, God was—and is—drawing hurting people to Himself.

It's this undying faith in God which creates a legacy that marches across time, fills up the books of the Bible, and creates heroes out of common, flesh-and-blood men and women. It's what causes Christian nuns in Calcutta to nurse their sick until they themselves succumb to disease, to lay down their lives for torture and death in order to preach the gospel, and to give their lives in sacrifice to one another.

We can't save souls. But we can lead suffering people to the One who can.

Because it never was about us, our families, or our children.

It has always been about the Lord.

Only He can heal for eternity. Only He was worthy to offer His life as a perfect and sinless sacrifice, so that we might draw near to a holy God. Only He can save, and only He can give eternal life that will not fade, will not allow pain or suffering, and will never pass away.

God has promised to "wipe every tear from our eyes" (Revelation 21:4) and to throw death, once and for all, into the lake of fire where it belongs.

In the meantime, He is working even through events as terrible as tornadoes, hurricanes, and ice storms, to draw people into His tender, loving arms.

3. CHOOSE TO RUN TO HIM RATHER THAN AWAY FROM HIM IN DISASTER.

Another couple who can testify to God's goodness is Simon and Athena Delgado, both age 37. Athena is an early education teacher and Simon installs cable lines. Their youngest two kids, Haley, age 8 and Xavier, age 9, miraculously survived the collapse of Plaza Towers Elementary. Their oldest son, Adrian, was out of school for a doctor's appointment, so he huddled in the closet with Simon and Athena while the tornado passed by the house they'd just started renting. Marissa, the eldest daughter, was safely sheltered in the High School.

"The noise and the pressure [from the atmosphere] were almost unbearable. We held each other close," Athena recalls. "My husband told us, 'Don't let go, no matter what,' and my son kept chanting, 'We're going to be okay, we're going to be okay.' I kept praying for God to take away the noise because it was so loud. Then, it stopped...everything. I was so scared to get out of my closet. I was convinced all that was left was the closet."

While the Delgados' home was still standing, their entire neighborhood and streets were clogged with debris, rubble, and downed power lines. Athena remembers it distinctly as they rushed outside, trying desperately to navigate the ruined streets to make it to Plaza Towers Elementary. "The smell of gas consumed every breath I took, and the sight of a house on fire sent terror through my body," she says. "When my husband pointed out where our old house had been, I was in complete disbelief. The idea that it was once a house was unimaginable."

The closer they got to the school, the more difficult the roads became until they finally had to jump out of the car and run to the school on foot.

"I was so disoriented I did not know where I was or where I was standing. I started yelling, 'I'm looking for my kids; I'm looking for my kids!'" remembers Athena. "A man asked me what grade, and I told him both second and third grade. His face changed at that moment, and I knew I did not want to hear the next words out of his mouth. The man said, 'The second graders are up front, and the third graders are right there.' The world stopped spinning in that brief moment when I watched his fingers point to the rubble. My son was buried. I broke down and prayed in the arms of a stranger." Fearing for Xavier's life, Athena prayed, "I can handle anything that might be wrong with him, just please give me one more day with my son.'"

As people dug through the rubble, they found nine year old Xavier. Alive. A ceiling tile had impaled his back and side, so the Delgados grabbed their daughter Haley, already retrieved from the school with minor injuries, and they rushed Xavier to the hospital.

Athena remembers how Xavier was upset about his friend Christopher Legg, "As we were carrying him to the car, Xavier was talking to me and saying, 'Mommy, I kept hollering Christopher's name and he wouldn't answer me, I think he was dead.'"

Xavier was right, Christopher Legg, age nine, didn't make it out. Nicolas McCabe, also one of Xavier's best friends, had passed away in the rubble right next to Xavier. Five other kids were lost as well, all in the same hallway, the same class, each with heartbreaking stories and loving families.

Unlike Principal Amy Simpson, Athena didn't really consider herself a true Christian believer. Like many Oklahomans, she went to church growing up, but God didn't mean much to her. "I just went to church sometimes and prayed when things got tough," she said. "After the tornado, though, the pain of everything was deep. Everything inside me changed. I started drinking every night when I got home, not to get drunk but just to make the tightness I felt in my chest loosen a little. People at work stopped talking to me or maybe I stopped talking to them, who knows."

It was a time of pain, of searching, of questions without answers.

Athena wrestled with the pain and uncertainty of it all. The memories of Xavier's distress in calling repeatedly for Christopher and his sadness for the loss of his other friends – these things haunted her. She was angry that her kids were no longer innocent. They'd seen destruction and death.

Eventually, Athena was forced to deal with the emotions she couldn't heal on her own. She credits Scripture with helping to bring about the first changes.

One of many great outreaches that came to Moore after the disaster was called the "Hope Station." This was set up at the site where the school collapsed and at the location of the informal temporary memorial site. Athena met people from all over the country who came there to help, pray, and support the city of Moore. "It was all the different people from all over the world coming to pray for us and with us." She says, "I wanted to know what they had that I didn't have. I remember getting a T-shirt and wanting to write a Bible verse on it, but I didn't know any verses. So I flipped the Bible open, landing in Psalms and kept reading, almost forgetting about the shirt. I guess that lit the flame of spiritual interest. I shyly visited Elevate Church wanting and needing to hear more. Now here I am, so far from where I want to be but confident that God has huge plans for me if I just trust in Him even when things feel like they are falling apart."

As they continued to attend church, Athena's entire family, one by one, began to open up to the knowledge of God and their need for Him, and they've each made professions of faith in Jesus Christ. None of them are the same.

As their pastor, I've seen them change completely. Athena and Simon are actively discipling their kids, and they regularly bring lost people to church to hear the gospel. They serve the community and church in every way. They are different people now after meeting Jesus.

In fact, Simon, 37, now a cable, phone, and internet installer, has begun sharing his faith in Jesus with so many others that I periodically run into people who have been impacted by him. Take yesterday, for example. I spoke at the Jesus House, which is a homeless shelter for people diagnosed with mental illness. A woman approached me afterwards and asked if I was the pastor of Elevate Church.

"I am," I replied.

"Do you know Simon Delgado?" she asked me.

"Yes."

"Simon was my boss when he worked for Taco Bell," the woman explained. "He encouraged me to get my life right with the Lord and get straightened out. He prayed for me and talked openly about faith. Would you please tell him that I'm here, and that I'm finally making steps in the direction of changing my life? I want him to know I'm doing better and I'm on the road to recovery."

Oh yes. I will tell him.

"That's a perfect example of how it's different for me now," says Simon. "Before, I probably would have ignored a situation where someone's life had spun out of control. Now I see what God has done in our lives, and I'm not afraid to share His love with those who feel unloved."

As for Athena, she compares new faith and courage in Christ to living with a "bulletproof vest."

"No matter how bad things get in this life, I have the protection of the Lord, reassuring me that the eternal life He has for me is beyond even my wildest imagination," Athena explains. "I don't have to understand why we go through hard times in life. It's just having faith that His plan is always with purpose."

Oddly enough, it was a tornado that God used to draw Simon and Athena to Himself. It was suffering, grief, and fear that He used to tenderly speak to their children. It was the shake-up of their day-to-day lives, and the "new normal" that impacted them deeply.

Athena quotes Romans 8:28 when she recalls that fateful day: "And we know that God causes all things to work together for good to those who love God, to those who are called according to His purpose."

The Delgados offer a list of things they are thankful for, things they believe represent God's provision from that day:

» That they left the Medical Center early enough that day to miss the destruction there.

» That they didn't take shelter at their old home, which they were moving out of the same day.

» For Xavier's teacher Mrs. Jennifer Doan-Rogers who wrapped her arms around him and another child. She broke her back and sternum and could have lost the child she was carrying.

» For the teacher, Mrs. Shelley Calvert who protectingly cradled tiny Haley in her arms.

» For God speaking to them and drawing their entire family to Himself through this difficulty.

Psalm 66:8-12 says it like this:

Praise our God, all peoples,
let the sound of his praise be heard;
he has preserved our lives
and kept our feet from slipping.
For you, God, tested us;

you refined us like silver.
You brought us into prison
and laid burdens on our backs.
You let people ride over our heads;
we went through fire and water,
but you brought us to a place of abundance.

God will always lead us to a place of abundance. Whether through life drawn closer to Him through pain, or through death and into the eternal Eden, we will find abundance if we trust Him.

It is God who cradles wounded children's hearts, meets our deepest needs, encourages grieving parents and chaplains, and rains down revival on a lonely, storm-battered part of town. It is God who orchestrates moments and meetings, and calls out to the broken to lean on Him.

For God as our Father has already suffered through everything we could endure, specifically through the loss of His beloved child and the pain and suffering of His now cursed Creation.

Jesus Christ was even tempted by Satan to give up the quest to save humanity. Yet because of His great love for us, He did not.

Our God is a loving Father who brings life from the rubble when we have given up hope.

Moments of joy appear when we least expect them, showing us again and again that God is good. Like Athena and Amy and Bunny, we realize—slowly, perhaps, in tiny and painful steps that God can be trusted, and God is always at work on behalf of the sons and daughters He dearly loves. Like Sam Porter, the disaster relief hero, we come to understand that no disaster is too devastating for God to bring good.

Like the first tender leaves that unfurl through the ashes, He brings the miracle of growth and new life, if we will let Him.

For He alone sees the whole picture, start to finish.

To hear more about faith in the face of natural disasters use the QR code below or go to www.WhereWasGod.com/book.

6

ILLNESS AND DISABILITY

JESUS IS ONBOARD YOUR SHIP

That day when evening came, he said to his disciples, "Let us go over to the other side." Leaving the crowd behind, they took him along, just as he was, in the boat. There were also other boats with him. A furious squall came up, and the waves broke over the boat, so that it was nearly swamped. Jesus was in the stern, sleeping on a cushion. The disciples woke him and said to him, "Teacher, don't you care if we drown?" He got up, rebuked the wind and said to the waves, "Quiet! Be still!" Then the wind died down and it was completely calm.

- Mark 4:34-39 -

It was 2012, the twentieth wedding anniversary for my wife Chrysty and me. The two of us, along with our five kids, were in a cruise ship's five-star dining room for a formal meal, celebrating, when it happened.

I glanced over just as Chrysty started leaning forward over the table. Her face was noticeably distressed, with her mouth slightly open but no sound coming out. She grabbed at her throat. Seeing the color fade from her face, my questions gave way to understanding. Something was terribly wrong. Confusion and fear swirled in my head. Time slowed.

She wasn't breathing.

Chrysty had been having some intermittent physical problems lately. She'd even had a few brief spells with difficulty swallowing, but nothing like this.

As emergencies cement themselves in our memories, I distinctly remember my thought process - from realization, to horror, then to feeling a slight bit of peace as I thought, "Okay God, is this how You're going to take her?" In that instant, I looked up and saw my two youngest kids across the table: Mikayla, then age 12, and Jeremy, age 10. In their faces and eyes I've never seen such fear. This wasn't only about me and my precious bride. What would this do to the kids?

"Dear God!" my heart cried out. "Don't let this happen. Please don't let the kids watch their mom die!"

Because of Chrysty's illness and the way it's wounded our family, this chapter is intensely personal for me. We are still walking through this valley of illness and physical distress with Chrysty—with joy and trust, yes, but also with desperate grief. Our emotions are raw, sometimes overflowing. Our hopes are raised until, a few days later, we feel them sputter out again, like mist on a smoldering fire, and we plunge back into the dark moments of, "Why, God?" and, "Why

Chrysty? Why this, and why now?"

Our struggle is real. It is happening now. And it hurts.

Illness, disability, and physical ailments are a unique type of storm because they strike at our very bodies; the flesh we depend upon to tie our shoes, lift a spoon, and swallow.

Have you ever heard the saying, "If you have your health, you have everything?"

Conversely, when you don't have good health, or legs that cooperate, or asthma-free lungs that rush fresh oxygen to your blood cells, you may feel like you've lost everything.

Remember Job, the God-fearing man of the Bible whom Satan struck with blow after tragic blow in order to prove that Job would abandon his faith? After Satan attacked Job's flocks and herds, his income and livelihood, the lives of his children, there was one final step in Satan's attack.

> "Skin for skin!" Satan replied. "A man will give all he has for his own life. But now stretch out your hand and strike his flesh and bones, and he will surely curse you to your face." The Lord said to Satan, "Very well, then, he is in your hands; but you must spare his life." So Satan went out from the presence of the Lord and afflicted Job with painful sores from the soles of his feet to the crown of his head. Then Job took a piece of broken pottery and scraped himself with it as he sat among the ashes" (Job 2:4-8).

What is the thing that Satan viewed as the last straw, the final hold-out, or the "death blow," if you will, for Job's faith? It wasn't his money. It was his own health. His own body. His own skin.

Because it's that personal.

In a family meeting in summer 2014 to talk about what details we felt comfortable sharing in this book, I found out just how traumatic this three-year-old event—Chrysty's choking episode on that cruise ship—was for my five kids. Chrysty's illness has had a huge impact on our family. All of us have struggled with God and faith because of it; several of us more than others. But all of us have hurt.

"I remember when mom was choking," said Jeremy, my youngest son, now 13. "I was thinking, 'This isn't happening. We're just a normal family." As the tears slowly crept into his eyes, he told us, "I remember feeling like God wasn't there at all."

John-Mark, my oldest son, now 16, picked up where Jeremy left off. "When I saw her and thought she was going to die. I thought, 'This can't happen to us.'"

Kimmy is our second daughter, 20 years old now. Her initial response was raw. "I was pretty angry until I realized that God obviously put the ER doctors at the table right next to us."

She was right. There we were, in the middle of a cruise ship dining hall. The concierge was asking what he could do to help, awkwardly fluttering about. At one point, he said in his thick Romanian accent, "Don't worry, I can never let you die in my restaurant!" Water boys handed us napkins and more water, as my precious bride of twenty years slowly went unconscious, the rest of the well-dressed diners staring at her.

"For the longest time, it was like God didn't even care, but if those doctors hadn't have been at the table next to us, she would have died," Kimmy continued. "So it was like, oh, maybe He does care. He's still taking care of us."

And she was right. In God's Divine providence, *He had seated our family right next to a table full of ER doctors.* How often does that happen? They leapt up from their table and sprang into action, dislodging the food from Chrysty's throat and saving her life.

Mikayla, our youngest daughter, now 14, was more pointed in her comments. "Why would this happen to us? Why would God let this happen to a family? Why *our* family?" By this time, our family meeting to talk about this book had become a sob-fest. Mikayla continued, "I don't understand. We believe in God and live for Him. Why would He let this happen to us?"

Her questions resonated with us all. *This isn't supposed to happen to us!* Our inner sense of fairness was challenged.

Why me? This happens to other people, but not us. Not this. Not now.

For us, that day on the cruise ship was only the beginning of the painful, heart-wrenching path we've walked as a family, watching my beloved Chrysty struggle with her health, even her very life.

Everything started in the months leading up to July 5, 2007. Chrysty had experienced a few strange physical spells: some blurred vision, flu-like symptoms a few times, dizziness, a lack of balance, and a host of other seemingly unrelated symptoms. They never stayed long enough for doctors to suggest any serious problems.

But then on the July 4 of that year, we spent a day of "family quality time" working on one of our rental properties. Our family is close, and we have a culture of teamwork. I didn't give it much thought when we went out in the 100-degree heat and worked a long, hard day.

The next day, what we knew as our "normal lives" would change forever. Chrysty was unable to get out of bed. She couldn't move one of her legs at all. She was dizzy and unbalanced. One of her eyes was blurred badly.

In the coming weeks Chrysty muddled through doctor visits, MRIs, and making simple trips to the bathroom, but she didn't improve.

Instead, she worsened. We helped feed her. She couldn't hold a spoon or cut up her own food.

These initial days were exhausting. We sought multiple opinions. We scoured the internet for solutions. We poured our savings into alternative treatments, feverishly looking for a solution. We stumbled onto an ugly diagnosis: multiple sclerosis, which was progressing fast and could cut short her life.

Multiple sclerosis? This couldn't be happening to Chrysty, not at age 33, a vibrant pastor's wife and mother.

"Other than shock, I was determined in the beginning to find a solution, to find out what I needed to do and do it," Chrysty says. "We would tackle and conquer it. Like everything else we'd ever done as a family."

But this time, we learned how little control we had over life.

One of the top neurologists in the region told us plainly, "She may recover from this episode, but others will come. They will increase. They can attack any part of the body. She'll probably end up in a wheelchair within a few years. Then who knows past that." He went on to let us know that there's no cure, that seeking alternative forms of healing wouldn't help, and that given this case, "there really isn't much hope of recovery."

It has been seven years now, and it's been a slow disappointment with reality. My precious bride has not recovered. I can compare a recent photo of myself with one from just four years ago, and I realize that I'm aging faster than I did previously.

This ongoing illness has been more taxing for us than the death of several close mentors, our grandparents and even the tragic self-inflicted death of Chrysty's dad. With this illness, we simply don't know if Chrysty might wake up one morning unable to move certain parts of her body. We don't know if she may have a surprise flare-up that causes her to choke on food and end her life. When she has a flare-up, we don't know if she'll recover or how long recovery might take or to what extent she may or may not recover.

When the darkness of the illness arrives, sometimes because of the cognitive struggles, I feel the love of my life slipping away. I mourn when our shared memories drift from her. Sadness overwhelms me when I recall her graceful dance movements and perfect posture from days past, and see her now unable to sit up or smile as she once did.

Has your heart ever mourned with similar feelings of longing and loss? Or possibly even felt abandoned by the Lord? Throughout history, every one has experienced storms, tragedy, trauma or disappointment. I'm sure those who are honest will admit to similar emotions.

"This isn't supposed to happen to us!" - Can you hear this heart cry felt by Jesus' disciples as their boat was filling with water one day on the Sea of Galilee?

We get a glimpse of the terror felt by the disciples during this particularly drastic storm.

Being at sea was the perfect escape for Jesus and his disciples. Many of them were fishermen, skilled, professional, strong. There's no doubt if they'd had any clue about the storm that was to come, they would have waited before heading out.

But sometimes you can't see what's coming in life.

The disciples likely knew well this area. The Sea of Galilee was 13 miles long and 8 miles wide in a valley, so at times a storm could appear before you knew it was coming. The area was known for sudden raging storms. Mark writes, "A furious squall came up..."

Some of life's storms are sudden. Unexpected. The types of struggles that we cannot be prepared for. Some words carry a devastating impact.

Just this week, a beloved staff member from our church was at a routine prenatal visit when she heard words that changed her reality. "I'm so sorry, I can't find the baby's heartbeat. I don't know what happened." And her hopes, dreams, future, and expectations are changed forever. Another perhaps hears the dreaded word "cancer" and everything changes with a simple but "furious squall."

"I remember feeling like God wasn't there at all..." The words of my youngest son echo in my head as I try to put myself in the position of these rough fishermen.

Maybe the skeptics are right. Maybe faith is a crutch for the weak. Maybe there's nothing to it. Or maybe if God is there He simply doesn't care.

Where was Jesus when this violent storm sent beads of water like missiles driving into their arms and backs? Where was Jesus as the waves pounded the shell of the boat?

The author Mark gives us the answer, "Jesus was in the stern sleeping on a cushion."

After the work He was expected to do, Jesus feel into a deep slumber. The disciples were struggling to control the boat, I'm sure grabbing whatever was available to scoop out the water. They pulled and struggled to keep the boat above the waves, and Jesus slept while the rest were terrified.

"Teacher, don't you care if we drown?!"

Don't you even care? God, don't You even care when life abuses us in ways that impact our physical bodies? We feel that You've designed us for a purpose here on this Earth. Everything we'll accomplish here will be done in this one body that You've given us.

While my family's journey has taken a toll on us, there are good things we've been given, too, much like the brilliance of sunshine through rain.

Here are a few things we've learned as a family, and a few ways we've grown in the midst of our storms:

COMPASSION MUSCLES DEVELOP AS WE SUFFER WELL.

We get at least a hint of what compassion means when we see in several places in the gospel the expression that Jesus was "*moved with compassion*." (An example is Matthew 14:14, but there are a number of other places.) He didn't just "feel" or "experience" compassion, He was moved by it.

This movement is what might separate compassion from simply feeling sorry for someone. The ability to empathize with those who are hurting is a valuable tool.

The word itself gives us more insight. Compassion comes from the Latin: com—with, passion–suffering. Compassion literally means to suffer with someone else. Empathizing with others. Putting ourselves into the shoes and experiences of those who struggle.

Early in my ministry and marriage, I could have given you this definition. I would have been partially right, but my understanding today is far deeper than before. St. Augustine addressed this exact sentiment when he wrote, "By stretching [a wineskin or sack] therefore, you increase the capacity of the sack, and this is how God deals with us. Simply by making us wait, He increases our desire, which in turn enlarges the capacity of our soul, making it able to receive what is to be given to us."

Not long ago, I remember seeing my boys jump out of our Suburban.

One of them grabbed the wheelchair from the back. The other opened the door for his mom and tenderly took her purse, helping her out of the seat and transferring her into the chair. Thinking of it now, I'm struck by the profundity: *Chrysty's illness has developed some incredible capacity for compassion in my kids!*

But it's not only compassion for their mom. Each of my children has been quick to look out for those in need. Opening doors. Giving a helping hand. Smiling with a bit more sincerity. Being quick to offer comfort rather than criticism when someone experiences difficulty.

I can see in their hearts and lives what C. S. Lewis meant when he wrote in his important book, *Problem of Pain*, "What is good in any painful experience is, for the sufferer, his submission to the will of God, and, for the spectators, the compassion around the acts of mercy to which it leads."[24]

It's not just my kids—it's me, too. My own sensitivity to people who are hurting is heightened. I find myself continually trying to see what is behind the eyes of people I meet. Are there hidden pains they are experiencing? What sorrow has he known? What struggle has she suffered? In what way might I learn from this person's pain or even minister to them in it?

I've also noticed that as my compassion has increased, so has my brokenness.

When I use the term "broken" I'm not referring to the type of brokenness that one needs to heal, or being broken like a plastic child's toy a few days after Christmas. The brokenness I'm referring to is a simple recognition that I'm not in control, but God is. Brokenness is knowing my limitations and pressing forward anyway. Godly brokenness is having confidence in Christ rather than myself.

24 *Problem of Pain*, C.S. Lewis (New York: HarperOne, 1996), 110.

Brokenness indicates increased vulnerability with myself, with the Lord, and with others. It's healthy because it promotes actual emotional and spiritual health by acknowledging rather than denying pain. It's positive because I can only overcome what I acknowledge. It's encouraging because with increased awareness of my weakness, comes increased awareness of His strength.

Check out what the Psalmist says about brokenness "The sacrifice you desire [Lord] is a broken spirit. You will not reject a broken and repentant heart, O God" (Psalm 51:17 NLT).

According to Scripture, brokenness seems to be the only healthy response to our own sinfulness. But not only to our own sinfulness, but also to the pain and suffering that our broken world can cause. If we can allow our hearts to be broken, experience genuine mourning, and run to Jesus for the healing that only He can bring, then our hearts can be transformed.

Are you wounded by physical ailments? Is someone close to you walking through a hard time with their physical body? Would you consider taking the pieces of your broken hearts and carrying them to Jesus?

God wants to use your pain to sharpen you, to help you grow and develop, and to expand your compassion as a result of your struggle.

FAMILIES CAN GROW CLOSER DURING HARD TIMES.

Alyssa, my oldest daughter, was away at college. Kimmy, our second daughter, was in her last high school year. Between their maturing and leaving the nest and Chrysty's declining health, we didn't know how many chances we'd get to be together on a trip. So for Thanksgiving we rented a cabin, loaded up, and headed towards the beautiful Colorado mountains. Coming from the flatlands of Oklahoma, the snow caps and crisp air of Colorado were glorious.

With Chrysty's health issues, though, trips can be complicated. We need more space for her "chariot." Frequent rest stops. Searching for wheelchair-accessible hotels. But after all the practice, Team Earp (as we affectionately call ourselves) was getting better working together as we took off into the Colorado mountains. Sometimes, it was like a well-oiled machine. When needed, we'd make stops on the trip. The girls would jump in to help Mom. The boys would move things around, clean up, gas up, or whatever else we needed.

Then we arrived at the Royal Gorge—a one-thousand foot splendor with red granite walls descending into a deep, rocky crevice, and a silver river cutting through the bottom. A single slender bridge hovered across it all, like a silky strand of a spider web. We couldn't wait to get up there.

Except for one thing.

Everywhere we looked, posted signs shouted, "Trails Not Wheelchair Accessible!" When we wheeled Chrysty up toward the gorge, Jeremy, my youngest said, "Not wheelchair accessible? I guess they don't know much about Team Earp!"

It was decided. Whatever difficulties this "non-accessible" trail held, we would conquer it. Wheelchair and all.

Still now on quiet nights, I might be able to feel the muscle soreness from that day! This three-quarter-mile section was filled with steps, gravel, rocks, and grades so steep that it was nearly at a 45 degree angle, but everyone jumped in. We pushed, pulled, carried, and struggled our way, as a family, to the end line.

We looked down through the plummeting emptiness together, taking in the slant of the sun on the jagged rocks, seeing the dizzying depth of the gorge, and feeling the breaths of cool air that wafted up from the canyon. The huge expanse of sky around us as we hung there almost suspended over all the blues and reds and browns.

We had done it. And we took turns taking pictures with us all standing around Chrysty in her wheelchair, next to a sign that says "Trails Not Accessible."

I can't think of anything that bonds people together quite like a shared struggle. Few things can build teamwork and camaraderie like suffering together. Celebrating the winning of games. Crying together at the losses. Shared experiences of tears and triumph. Tension and release. Ebb and flow.

This is one of the reasons many men and women who serve in the military together view themselves as brothers and sisters for life. Also, championship sports teams often have to go through pain and disappointment together before reaching their potential for teamwork. There are loads of studies on this topic.

"Shared pain may be an important trigger for group formation," said an article in the journal *Psychological Science*. Researcher and psychologist Brock Bastian of the University of New South Wales went on to say, "Pain, it seems has the capacity to act as social glue, building cooperation."[25]

It's bolstered by scientific experiments, too. Shared pain encourages solidarity, unity, and common experiences. This was true for Jesus' disciples.

No one would have expected Jesus' first disciples to achieve anything. Individually, they were mostly uneducated lower class. But Jesus took this ragtag group of hotheaded, rough-and-tumble men

---

25 "Shared Pain Brings People Together," *Association for Psychological Science*, September 9, 2014 (http://www.psychologicalscience.org/index.php/news/releases/shared-pain-brings-people-together.html, accessed July 18, 2015).

(who would have almost certainly been at odds with each other from the start) to change the world in the first century.

Matthew had been a tax collector for the enemy Roman government. Simon was the opposite, a "Zealot," part of an extreme religious political group that some feared would incite riots against the Romans. Most, like Peter and Andrew were fishermen. James and John bickered for the best places of honor. Thomas is still publicly known for doubting. The whole group argued together over who was the greatest, and Peter was so impetuous that after three years of serving with Jesus, he still thought God's plan was for them to take over the kingdom with a sword!

How did Jesus ever get them united?

Remember the storm? The furious squall?

As the waves crashed into the boat, these headstrong, confident and burly men were reduced to fearful, quivering children. Imagine as they glanced at each other during the storm - when they saw the terror in each other's eyes, they did not pass judgment. Instead, *they related to the others and affirmed the fear the others felt!* They may have locked arms or even embraced one another as they faced what they may have assumed was the end of life together.

Is it possible that this struggle was actually part of God's plan? Part of His plan to bring solidarity or unity to this group?

There's an interesting section in 1 Corinthians that comes to mind. Take a look at what Paul writes as he tells the Corinthian church about unity:

> "Just as a body, though one, has many parts, but all its many parts form one body, so it is with Christ. For we were all baptized by one Spirit so as to form one body—whether Jews or Gentiles, slave or free—and we were

> all given the one Spirit to drink. Even so the body is not made up of one part but of many" (1 Corinthians 12:12-14).

All the parts should have equal concern for each other. "If one part suffers, every part suffers with it," Paul writes in verse 26, "if one part is honored, every part rejoices with it."

There's no question our family has grown closer through our shared struggle. Not only because of our teamwork, but in a number of other ways.

Most of all, I pray that as my kids watch me love Chrysty—and serve the Master who created her—they'll be inspired. That one day, in their lives, when they are walking through difficulty, they'll look back and say, "Mom and Dad went through some hard times. But I know I can get through this, because they got through that!"

In every season of life, God is working on us. Growing us. Strengthening us. Bringing us to a place of spiritual depth where He can use us even more.

HARDSHIP CAN BRING ON EMOTIONAL AND SPIRITUAL DEPTH.

The most common question I'm asked when ministering to people in hardship is, "Is it wrong to question God?" I'm thankful when people ask this question. It indicates a rare and raw authentic journey as they consider their own hearts, and how their hearts relate to His.

The answer is plain. It is *not* wrong to ask God, "Why?" The disciples struggling in the sinking boat asked a similar question. In fact, it's possible that asking God, "Why?" could be the beginning of great spiritual and emotional growth.

Briefly scan the Psalms, and you'll see that many of them are heart cries. Bible teachers call them "laments." The psalmist writes his feelings without cleaning them up first. Without filtering them to make sure he uses the correct "church language."

Mikayla, my youngest daughter, now 15, shared recently about an experience she had a few years ago. "It was a Wednesday night and we [the family] were talking about going to the hospital and how the last time we went there, we had to convince Mom who Kimmy (our second daughter) was. I got out of the car and stormed off. I was praying, 'Why would you do this to my mom? She's always so positive and loving. Why her?'"

At this point, my tears started to match hers. How do I answer such longing? I'm the preacher-man, her daddy, and in the past I'd been her Bible-Answer-Man. But I just cried with no answers.

It was Chrysty who answered her. "You know, you can always cry out to God," she said to Mikayla. "He's the answer to all our problems. He knows why this is happening. He can take it when you ask questions like this. His shoulders are very large. Sometimes I myself even scream at Him, quietly in my head."

Yes, Chrysty, you're right. The shoulders of Jesus are so large and strong, able to carry the cross of suffering; able to handle questions from a young woman without judging her harshly; able to calm the storms on a raging sea when the boat is filled with terrified fishermen; able to care for us even as we question Him.

Maybe answers aren't what we need. Maybe what we need most is to have the courage to ask the hard questions. Chrysty's words reminded me of a psalm:

> "When I consider your heavens,
>   the work of your fingers,
> the moon and the stars,

which you have set in place,
what is mankind that you are mindful of them,
human beings that you care for them?" (Psalm 8:3-4).

Out of all the stars, the planets, and even the billions of people who have lived on this globe, what are we, that God is mindful of us? That He cares for us?

And does He even hear what I say when I question Him?

He does. And just as importantly, when we ask, we begin to listen. Actually, *questions can be the beginning of hearing His voice.*

It almost feels like a break through. Like getting a second wind. You push, you struggle, you endure, you cry out then at just the right moment, you actually hear His voice. You get some clear understanding like a lighting flash. Or a breakthrough in maturity. Or God sends someone at just the right moment speaking words you've asked about. Or you realize God is using you in an amazing way to speak life to someone else. But this great revelation and life in Christ doesn't happen while living a life of surface "belief" or shallow faith. You've got to press in to get it!

Hebrews 12:1-3 seems to address this very thing, even using the language of a runner, an athlete, driving towards the finish line. "And let us run with *perseverance*," it says. The original Greek word for "perseverance" is "hypomone"— "*to bear up under, endure, suffer patiently.*" A form of that word is translated once as "persevere" and twice as "endure."

Notice it here:

> "And let us run with ***perseverance*** the race marked out for us, fixing our eyes on Jesus, the pioneer and perfecter of our faith. For the joy set before him he ***endured*** the cross, scorning its shame, and sat down at the right hand

of the throne of God. Consider him who ***endured*** such opposition from sinners, so that you will not grow weary and lose heart."

Wow! In this text, God encourages us to "endure." We fix our eyes on Jesus as our example, because He himself "endured!" Why? So we "will not grow weary and lose heart!" Dear friend, if our Lord encourages us to endure, then He *will* equip us to do so! Hang in there. Press in. Persevere. Ask Him and see if He doesn't help you endure!

Suffering strengthens us. It helps us to see the condition of our hearts before the Lord. Suffering allows us to understand what the condition of our faith is for real, what our faith is like behind the mask of fakery that we so quickly wear. Author Tim Keller wrote about this in his book, *Walking with God through Pain and Suffering*. He said this: "Suffering reveals the impurities or perhaps the falseness of our faith in God. In a sense, it is only in suffering that faith and trust in God can be known to be in God, and therefore it is only in suffering that our love relationship with God can become more and more genuine."[26]

So does pain and suffering always result in growth and development? Unfortunately not. Many times we see people get *bitter* rather than *better*. It's easy to slide into apathy or passivity rather than pressing in and squeezing every drop of growth out of the experiences life throws at us.

So, then, the tools for developing inner strength must be inner life tools. It may differ person to person, but here are some things we've found helpful as a family:

Journaling – Keep a spiritual journal. Share your inner life with yourself. Write out prayers or Scripture or both. You can see how you've changed over time.

---

26 *Walking with God through Pain and Suffering*, Tim Keller (New York: Penguin, 2013), 192.

Solitude and silence – Ruth Haley Barton says, "Solitude at its most basic and profound level, is simply an opportunity to be ourselves with God."[27] Quiet times of reflection are essential to get to know ourselves and our Master better. They help us dig a deep well of positive emotional resources that we can draw from during times of struggle.

Seeking God, relentlessly – It's only by seeking that we find Him. Thomas Merton's writings have been helpful to me in seeing God transform my inner life. He says of seeking, "Inner silence depends on a *continual seeking*, a continual crying in the night, a repeated bending over the abyss... For He is found when He is sought, and when He is no longer sought, He escapes us."[28]

Community – Find mature people who have suffered and suffered well. Seek out those who have endured pain, but still trust Jesus and love people.

Art – Whether music, poetry, prose or some other art form, we find that art speaks the language of the heart. It can bypass the weaknesses of our sometimes critical mind and minister directly to deep places within us that cause us to long for the otherworldly reality that is Jesus.

Safe, Open Sharing – For us, we've found this both with other ministry professionals and within our own family. Whatever you can't talk about controls you, so it's essential to find a place to share your heart safely. Find a mature person of God to help you unpack your inner life or possibly look for a professional—a good Christian counselor, maybe, or a grief group can be life-changing.

Watching A Hero Suffer Well – One of our biggest blessings has

---

27 *Invitation to Solitude and Silence: Experiencing God's Transforming Presence*, Ruth Haley Barton (Downers Grove, IL, 2004), 136.

28 As quoted in the book, *Invitation to Solitude and Silence: Experiencing God's Transforming Presence*, Ruth Haley Barton (Downers Grove, IL, 2004), 85.

been my wife, even in times when she struggles to remember basic things. She loves us and loves Jesus with everything she is. This has changed the rest of the family and it has changed many others around her.

Recently, our oldest daughter Alyssa reflected on how our struggle impacts her. "The biggest thing that has helped me with my faith and her illness has been watching Mom the past few years," she says. "I've grown just by watching her. She never wavers in her faith."

I agree! Watching someone slowly lose control of her body, and still trust Jesus and love the rest of us well—that creates change in me.

ILLNESS FORCES US TO SLOW DOWN AND APPRECIATE LIFE.

We've been open about our struggles as a family, about our faith, and about the process of God growing us up. As I'm so open about our experiences, it may seem as though our lives are dark, sad, and foreboding, especially as it relates to the storm of this chronic illness.

But if you follow us around, this isn't what you'll find. You won't pick up a negative, sad vibe being around our family. If you spent a week in our home, you'd hear much laughter daily, joking, teasing, funny stories, and excitement. If you were a guest at our weekly "family night" of dinner and games, you'd know that our lives are colored with the brightness of day much more than the darkness of night.

Just this past week, I spoke at the Jesus House of Oklahoma City, a shelter ministry for homeless people wrestling with diagnosed mental health issues. They wanted us to talk about how we deal with our life storm and still function day to day. Specifically, they wanted to know about what Chrysty and I call "The Box."

The "MS Box" is an imaginary place we store our feelings, hurts, and experiences; we open it and talk plainly about everything. Nothing is off limits, including the past, present, and future. Questions like, *How can I be a better dad through this? How can I love you kids better? How can I lead in a more spiritually healthy way?*

We discuss it all. Then we wrap it back up, put the box on the shelf, and live our lives and celebrate the excitement of all God is doing in us! This has helped me especially to learn to appreciate the seemingly small blessings in life.

There are many small things that I used to overlook. The beauty of nature is one.

"The greatness of the horizon and vastness of time and space screams silently that there's an artist painting on the canvas of the great expanses," I wrote in my journal a few years ago. *"Today, help me to 'pour forth' your glory just as effectively as do the soulless creations that are so obedient to profess You."*

Michael and Ryan McLaughlin of Oklahoma City lost their sweet daughter Ellie Kate to NKH (nonketotic hyperglycinemia) just after her seventh birthday. They have found joy in the "little things" as they and their three young children cope with all the changes in their family.

"I think all of us have a greater appreciation for the little things, definitely more than we might have had otherwise," says Ryan, a full-time mom who keeps a tremendously beautiful and powerful blog celebrating Ellie Kate's dazzling little life (wonderfullymadelife.blogspot.com). Ryan goes on to say, "After Ellie Kate died, I really felt that we needed to enjoy life. God gave us life on this earth, and He wants us to have life that is abundant!"

Nature is especially important, says Ryan, as well as driving around to places near them antiquing, picnicking, and hiking. Since the McLaughlins' younger daughter, Lucy, was also diagnosed with

NKH, it's even more essential to give their family quiet, rest, space, and joy.

"It's interesting to me that it took Ellie's death to get me to the point of truly seeking out enjoyment in life and in our surroundings," she says. "Before, I think, we were too caught up in survival mode (doctor's appointments, things to pick up at the store, home health care equipment being delivered), but I'm forever grateful that we have tiptoed out of that."

The younger version of me never enjoyed nature in the way that I do now. I didn't understand how "the heavens declare the glory of God" (Psalm 19:1) until I was forced to slow down.

Silence is another "not so small" thing of which I was previously unaware. But now, there are times I can actually agree with the psalmist when he said, "My soul silently waits for God alone; My salvation comes from Him. He alone is my rock and my salvation; He is my stronghold; I will never be shaken" (Psalm 62:1-2).

So today, when I'm walking in the Spirit of God and understanding, I look forward to simple things: A good day. A flower. A meal with the family. A day when my precious Chrysty feels well enough to let me roll her around the block in her wheelchair. Visiting the zoo.

I didn't use to enjoy these things. I was too busy. Life was too pressing. My task list was too important. How on earth would the world ever function if I didn't stay on my important task list?

Now, though, those moments are everything. The love I have for Chrysty is indescribable. What I once viewed as common is now made holy.

It is all holy—the suffering and the rejoicing—because we are consecrated for a holy God. We were created for eternity. And one day, every wrong will be made right, every injustice corrected, every tear will be wiped away. My bride will have a new body. No more wheelchair.

No more multiple sclerosis. No more tears.

One of the most brilliant expressions representing the reality of Christ, finality, and life comes from Tolkien's book, *The Lord of the Rings.* [29]

"Gandalf!" exclaims the Hobbit Sam Gamgee to the wizard. "I thought you were dead! But then I thought I was dead myself. Is everything sad going to come untrue?"

The answer is yes.

I weep just thinking of it.

Done. The whole deal.

This is the whole of the historic Christian message. Whatever you're experiencing now is temporary.

Find comfort in the small blessings. Learn what you can from any trial that comes your way. Grow and develop in ways that inspire others to greatness and overcoming. And realize that right now, you're in the middle of a great narrative story. You can't see the end, but you can have confidence in this.

In the end, dear Christian friend, you will find joy, peace, and the presence of God. Forever.

YOU CAN OVERCOME FRIENDLY FIRE WITH GRACE.

Many of our grieving or suffering friends have grown because of resistance training; learning to get past harsh statements made by well-meaning people who may not understand suffering or what the Bible says about it. TheGospelCoalition.org posted a great article and

---

29 *The Lord of the Rings*, J. R. R. Tolkien, (New York: Random House Publishing, 1966), 246.

interview about this topic on February 17, 2014. Pastor and writer Tullian Tchividijan said in this round table discussion, “Job’s friends were great counselors, until they opened their mouths.”[30]

Why is it that we seem to have this instinctive desire to want to “say something and just wrap a bow around life?” as Paul Tripp asked in the same discussion. Here are a few statements we should avoid when dealing with suffering people:

“I know how you feel.”

“Cheer up, He wouldn’t want you to be sad.”

“God will make something good about this.”

“Focus on the blessings.”

“It could be worse.”

“She’s in a better place.”

“God won’t give you more than you can handle.”

“Hasn’t it been long enough? Maybe it’s time to move on.”

“God will use this.”

SOMETIMES OUR ATTEMPTS TO HELP PEOPLE MAY ACTUALLY HURT THEM.

“I opened up my email and couldn’t believe what I was reading,” Rhett Burnett told me as he remembered the days and weeks surrounding his precious daughter Kraleigh’s death. “I guess this lady had read my blog about Kraleigh’s cancer, so she sent me pages and pages of scriptures telling me if I only ‘had enough faith’ then my daughter would be healed.”

---

30 Cited in “What Not to Say to Someone Who’s Suffering,” Matt Smethurst at thegospelcoalition.org (http://www.thegospelcoalition.org/article/what-not-to-say-to-someone-whos-suffering accessed July 29, 2015), February 17, 2014.

As Rhett continued to read the note, he found that the sender directly blamed Rhett for the fact that his daughter was not yet healed. This message heaped guilt, accusations, and added pain onto the hearts of these parents.

The hurtful message came during the very last week before Kraleigh went to Heaven, just days after the doctors told the Burnetts that nothing else could be done medically. Just imagine during such a difficult time for these parents, having someone they didn't even know accuse them of being responsible for their daughter's cancer... because their faith was too weak for Kraleigh to be healed by God.

Attacks like this are not uncommon. Many people who have experienced serious illness have had at least one similar encounter. Someone comes along, quoting scripture, believing they are following Jesus and determined to "set everyone straight." They either suggest or directly insist that healing is only out of reach because your faith isn't strong enough.

Probably these types of messages come from well-meaning folks who don't fully understand the scripture, or perhaps they've listened to the wrong televangelist and have been lead astray.

There are some people who assume it's always God's plan to heal every person, every time. This is simply not the case. Sometimes, in God's mysterious and gracious will, instead of giving us healing here on earth, He gives us the ultimate healing in Heaven, when we see Him face to face.

Am I saying that we shouldn't encourage people to pray for healing? Certainly not!

The New Testament is clear regarding healing. God is able! He can and does heal. (Matthew 8:2; Mark 10:16) We are to call on the elders of the church to anoint the sick with oil and to lay hands on them (James 5:14).

Early in my ministry, there was a toddler named Tritney. She had severe complications stemming from an allergic reaction to medication. The doctor had called in the family to say goodbye. He didn't expect Tritney to make it through the night. The family called a number of prayer warriors and elders from the church, and we cried out to Him. In just hours, by the time the family got to the hospital, the doctors told them it had to be a miracle—her symptoms were almost gone and they didn't see any reason to keep her there.

This was only the beginning of a journey with me regularly seeing instances of sicknesses, diseases, and afflictions of all kinds disappear with no explanation other than God's intervention.

But does He heal every person? In every case? Every time?

Clearly not. The very fact that we use the term "miracle" implies that they aren't common! The death rate is still 1:1, so even when God heals an ailment today, something else will arise to eventually kill the one who was healed! In this world, just as our suffering is temporary – our healing is also temporary.

Peter, one of the fishermen who survived the furious storm from Mark 4, knew much about suffering. He wrote in one of his New Testament letters, "So then, those who suffer according to God's will should commit themselves to their faithful Creator and continue to do good" (1 Peter 4:19).

Likewise, the Apostle Paul writes of the future hope. The hope that we do not yet fully possess.

> "...that the creation itself will be liberated from its bondage to decay, not only so but we ourselves, who have the first fruits of the Spirit, groan inwardly as we wait eagerly for our adoption to sonship, the redemption of our bodies.... We hope for what we do not yet have, we wait for it patiently" (Romans 8:21-25).

We do not yet have all the good things that are eventually coming to us, and this includes healing. Until we see Jesus face to face, we will always be left wanting more.

Admittedly, there is much tension in what I am sharing here. Where is the balance for those of us who pray fervently, believing God for healing, but still are left wondering if that healing will ever come?

Our family finds inspiration in the example set by three young Hebrew men named Shadrach, Meshach, and Abednego. They were condemned to die by the evil King Nebuchadnezzar because they refused to worship false gods. They were thrown into a blazing furnace to die. Just before being thrown in, they were given one more chance to reject God and serve idols. Their response gives me great strength. "If we are thrown into the blazing furnace, the God we serve is able to deliver us from it, and he ***will*** deliver us from your Majesty's hand. ***But even if he does not... we will not serve your gods...***" (Daniel 3:17-18).

We know the Bible teaches about supernatural healing in many scripture passages. We pray for healing. We trust God for healing. ***God can heal my precious bride, but if He doesn't, then we will still serve Him.***

Dear friend, if you're struggling with physical illness or disease, God has not left you. Your illness is not due to a "lack of faith." Your disease is part of the broken world we find ourselves in. God can heal you. He can deliver you! Cry out to Him and plead for it. But if in His sovereignty He does not heal you, know that one day you'll still be ultimately healed and delivered from this!

In the meantime, if people attack your faith with assertions that you yourself are responsible for your illness or the sickness of a loved one, know that you're in good company, and let that attack strengthen you as well.

REALIZE THAT GOD CARES DEEPLY, EVEN WHEN IT MAY NOT SEEM LIKE IT.

It can be frightful when you struggle with an illness or disease that causes your body to waste away prematurely, but even in that, you can always trust in the One who holds our lives.

The same God walks through it all with you—through every IV puncture, every loss of movement, every late night at the ER. While you're waiting on a cure, while you're waiting on healing, it isn't God turning away callously. He isn't ignoring you, and He does care. Far more than you think. It's a common misunderstanding when we assume that God doesn't care.

The disciples of Jesus made the same false assumption when they were in that storm on the Sea of Galilee. They asked, even as a sort of accusation, the same question that people suffering with Parkinson's and terminal cancer might want to ask. These guys had been following Jesus as He preached, helping Him heal the sick, and dealing with logistics of the crowds. They'd given up jobs, family, friendships, status, and basically everything they held dear to be with Jesus. Didn't they deserve better than Jesus *sleeping on a cushion* while they fought for their lives?

No wonder they woke Him in utter desperation. "Teacher," they cried in disbelief, "don't you care if we drown?"

Did you catch that? The confusion, the indignation, the crumpling pain?

"Teacher, don't you care?" (Mark 4:38).

"Don't you care that I'm in danger?"

"Don't you care about me at all?"

The emptiness of those words must have stabbed Jesus straight through the heart. After all those weeks and months together, the waking and walking, the breaking of bread, the close-knit moments when they learned secrets to the kingdom of God, the disciples still didn't get it. Interestingly enough, when that storm arose on the Sea of Galilee they didn't accuse Jesus of laziness or idleness. They didn't accuse Him of preaching so late into the evening that they caught the bad weather coming in across the hills. They accused Him of not caring.

Maybe the skeptics are right, we think. *Maybe faith is a crutch for the weak. Maybe there's nothing to it. Or maybe if God is there...He simply doesn't care.*

But here's the clincher: the whole reason Jesus was even in the boat with the disciples in the first place was because He *did* care! Infinitely. He cared so much about those struggling disciples—and all of us—that He left His heavenly kingdom and become a flesh-and-blood man to provide salvation. I mean, crucifixion? Really? How much would somebody have to mean to you in order for you to take their place on a gruesome torture chamber of a hill called Golgotha?

Jesus didn't just provide a place of safety for us, or a sanctuary from fear. He provided Heaven. He provided eternal health and perfect beauty that never fades. He provides a radiant crown instead of darkness, eternal life instead of eternal death, and peace with our holy creator God instead of the devil's hell.

Not only that, but the disciples had another reason not to fear: *Jesus was in the boat with them!* Did they really think the boat was going to go down in the Sea of Galilee with the Son of God sleeping inside? Granted, not all of them realized the extent of Jesus' power and Divine kingship; few of them, it seems, really grasped who Jesus was and why

He had come.

But they did know He had been sent by God, and they knew first-hand that He was a messenger of God on the level of Elijah. Peter was the one who got it right: "You are the Christ, the son of the living God" (Matthew 16:16).

What kind of God would sink His own boat? And what kind of God would make plans to "set out to the other side" and get waylaid into oblivion by a typhoon-like storm?

It sounds almost comical, but we do the very same thing!

We who are believers carry the presence of the living God with us *every single day* as a seal of our redemption__the "first fruits of the Spirit [which] groan inwardly as we wait eagerly for our adoption to sonship, the redemption of our bodies" (Romans 8:23).

We have been made alive by Christ, through Christ, with Christ. We are co-heirs, children of God, adopted sons and daughters, the dearly beloved of the Most High.

"Emmanuel," one of the names of Jesus predicted before His birth means literally "God with us," and we carry with us His precious promise that He will never leave us or forsake us. Never, not for a moment. Not even when it seems like His hand has slipped on the wheel (it hasn't), or when it feels like He's a thousand miles away (He isn't).

"I am with you always," He said to the disciples. To the same disciples who struggled in that water-laden, wind-battered boat. *Always! I am with you always!*

And He still says that to us today.

He is with us in the jostle and lights of the ER, in the physical therapy suite and the burn unit, in the stillness of the hospice room.

While our life seems to whip us around randomly, without any sense or meaning, and sometimes for long periods without any sign of the presence of God, we can know with all certainty that He is with us. He loves us. He cares deeply for us. He has always been with us.

We see his tender care in the simple fact that our storms are temporary.

It's easy for us to feel that our current pain, our current struggle, is permanent. But God will never allow any storm we face to afflict us forever. No storm lasts forever.

C. S. Lewis wrote it this way in his book *Perelandra:*

> "I'll tell you how to look at it. Haven't you noticed how, in our own little war here on earth, there are different phases, and while any one phase is going on people get into the habit of thinking and behaving as if it were going to be permanent? But really the thing is changing under your hands all the time, and neither your assets nor your dangers are the same as the year before."[31]

Life never stays the same. Ever.

Think back over the past decade of your life, and consider some of the storms you've sailed through and survived. How has God shown His faithfulness to you? How has He given you strength or helped you forgive, or how has He helped you go the extra mile in a hard situation you thought you couldn't bear anymore?

Shifting seas may change, and clouds may blow in, but your boat

---

31 C. S. Lewis, *Perelandra* (New York: Scribner, 1944), 22.

will not sink. Your storm will not last forever.

For those of you who still don't see a break in the storm and wind, hold on tight and keep looking for it. Just like the disciples, just like the McLaughlin family, just like my precious bride Chrysty, your story is not yet finished.

GOD CAN TURN YOUR GREATEST WEAKNESSES INTO YOUR GREATEST STRENGTHS.

You might be asking yourself this question: *What if the ending to my story isn't the one I hoped for? Would God still be good then?* What if Chrysty is never physically healed the way our family longs for? Can we still praise God even then and find Him faithful?

From cover to cover of the Bible, millions of voices cry out to us in thunderous unison: YES! Yes, God is abundantly faithful. Yes, God is good no matter what happens to us. *For His goodness does not depend on how the events of our lives play out.* His nature is wholly good. His plans for us are beyond anything positive we could ever imagine for ourselves.

Those who have experienced supernatural healing can attest to God's goodness and faithfulness no matter what. The martyrs who laid down their lives for the gospel would tell you yes, God is good, and His glorious will was accomplished in their lives. And in their deaths.

Maybe you don't directly relate to having your body broken or being someone's caregiver. But we can all relate to having limitations and shattered dreams.

One of my greatest heroes is LaTara Bussey. She suffered a different kind of physical devastation that's excruciating even to imagine. Yet she stands today as a testimony to God's love and faithfulness, and reminding us that what we imagine to be a limitation could very well be the exact thing God uses most greatly in our life and ministry.

"I experienced continual sexual molestation as early as three years old," says LaTara, 47, of Oklahoma City. "It started with a family member, then another one, then friends of the family. This went on until I was nine years old. You're looking for love and all you can relate it to is sex." [32]

LaTara's early life tragedies affected her view on life, sex, and self-worth for many years. The abused child transformed into a teen with self-esteem struggles, and as a young adult, she became the victim of extremely abusive relationships. At one low point, she sent her then five-year-old son, AJ, to live with her mother in Oklahoma when her Los Angeles-based business crashed. She lost her house. Her income stopped. LaTara became homeless.

"I first met the Lord when I was 20," she said, "but He really didn't become real to me until I was 39 years old and I tried to take my own life. AJ was on the other side of the room. I didn't even say it loud enough to be heard, but I said, 'Why even be here anymore?'"

Her young son AJ, after an inner prodding from the Lord, went over and snatched the scissors out of her hand. "God, what is wrong with me?" LaTara cried out.

At that moment the Bible passage Psalm 139:13-14 came to her mind. She didn't look it up for several days, but when she did, the words would change her forever. "For you [God] created my inmost being. You knit me together in my mother's womb. *I praise you because I am fearfully and wonderfully made; your works are wonderful, I know that full well.*"

"I just kept putting that scripture in my mind," LaTara says. "It

---

32 See the video testimony, "Why Be Here? God Answered" (http://elevatefaith.com/video/why-be-here-god-answered/ accessed February 15, 2015).

changed me. It reminds us that we're really a huge part of His plan."

That was the beginning of healing for her. LaTara learned to go back to the time when she was a three-year-old girl, abused, unloved, and alone. She learned to receive God's love, to love herself, and to love other people. Now, she uses her story to help bring healing to others. As a life coach, LaTara teaches people to order their lives so that they can bring out their greatest strengths and assets.

"It became real to me when I allowed God to show me my ugliest parts," she says. "I didn't like them, but I had to embrace them, so I could heal."

And after all those difficult years, LaTara began to experience a new life, and the abundance that Christ has even in the middle of darkness. Even after a tragedy. Even with an illness. Even through abuses. Even while going through the type of life storms that some tell us we should never recover from.

The most amazing thing for me about LaTara Bussey's story is that ***her greatest source of pain has become her greatest strength.*** Her pain is the very thing that propels her forward as God uses her to coach others. She continues to lead her sons in godliness; AJ as he ministers to people as a 22-year-old coach and youth pastor, doing missions in France and ministry in Oklahoma; and her youngest son Brahane as he transitions from boyhood to manhood.

Has God allowed LaTara and the Bussey boys to become great in spite of their struggles? Some might say so. I'd like to suggest instead that God has elevated them *because* of the problems they experienced.

The Bible is replete with stories of greatness that travel through a path of great suffering. The underdog who ended up as king. The girl nobody thought much about who gave birth to the King of Kings. Even the disciples, struggling there in the boat with Jesus. What was their greatest fear? Drowning? Suffering? Death? Why were they so afraid?

These were the same men who watched Christ from a distance as He was crucified, cowering in fear. Peter famously denied that he even knew Jesus three times! They were paralyzed by the thought of losing their lives.

And yet look at them later in life, when their days with Jesus had solidified into a faith that was amazing to behold. These men who had once fled in fear now proclaimed Christ boldly.

According to tradition, Peter was crucified upside-down. Other church traditions tell us about some of the early disciples who were crucified, speared to death, stoned, clubbed and burned alive. These first century Christians brought the good news of the gospel to Africa, Asia, and Europe, starting churches and baptizing believers whose successors remain even today. Many of them exhibit extraordinary faith they developed in spite of—or rather *because of*—their initial fears.

Chrysty, my precious bride, has discovered something extraordinary. Even in her weak body and sometimes impaired cognition, she says this: "I don't think that I'd want to go back to the way things were before. I've learned so much through this whole process... about me, about the rest of my family, about the Lord."

My precious bride has learned, through the hard art of suffering well, that Jesus Himself is in her boat, that her boat will not sink, and that her storm will not last forever.

And neither will yours.

Because in Christ's dying, He protected our living. He protected our future. He protected us from judgment and from hell.

And our living is beyond this place.

To hear more about LaTara Bussey's story and about the Earp family use the QR code below or go to www.WhereWasGod.com/book.

7

GRIEF AND LOSS

WE WERE NOT MADE FOR JUST THIS LIFE

Listen! Listen to the roar of his voice,
to the rumbling that comes from his mouth.
He unleashes his lightning beneath the whole heaven
and sends it to the ends of the earth.
After that comes the sound of his roar;
he thunders with his majestic voice.
When his voice resounds,
he holds nothing back.
God's voice thunders in marvelous ways;

he does great things beyond our understanding... Then the LORD spoke to Job out of the storm...

- Job 37:2a-38 -

When Scott McCabe of Moore, Oklahoma, had surgery at sixteen years old he woke up to some unusual news: he would never father a child.

McCabe, now 52, didn't think much of it at the time. He'd married twice before Stacey, all with no children, and it didn't seem to make much difference in his life. But when Stacey found out she was pregnant at the age of 40, neither Scott nor Stacey could believe it.

"I was elated," says Scott. "I was so happy. And when I told my parents, my mom and dad flipped out. They didn't think they would ever get a grandson."

They adjusted as quickly as they could to the news. Baby Nicolas McCabe arrived so quickly that first responders helped deliver him in the street in front of the McCabe's house before they could even head to the hospital.

Despite Scott and Stacy's shock and surprise at unexpected parenthood together, their first years as Nicolas' parents were sheer joy.

There was teething and swimming and school, and Nicolas pestering the cat, rambunctious laughter, and what Scott affectionately calls "orneriness." Like the day Nicolas didn't want to wear his swim shoes, and they fought over it all afternoon. Or all the times he bugged Scott and Stacey for extra snacks and snack money for school.

Nicolas, a happy brown-eyed boy who'd never met a stranger,

seemed to instinctively sense what was on his parents' hearts.

"He always knew when I was having a bad day," recalls Scott. "He would tell me, 'Daddy, it'll be all right.'"

But more than the fun and energy, there was love.

"I told Nicolas every day that I loved him," says Scott. "My dad never told me that he loved me. I knew he did, but he never said it. So I made a point of saying it every day. He would walk up to me in my chair, and he'd hug my neck and say, 'I love you, Daddy.' Then he'd go out there and start pestering his mom. He had a big heart."

Life had never been sweeter.

Until that day in 2013, when the now infamous tornado ripped through Moore and toppled the walls of Plaza Towers Elementary School where Nicolas huddled with his frightened classmates.

Scott and Stacey McCabe kissed Nicolas goodbye that morning for school and never saw him alive again.

When they tell the story of Nicolas' death, it's hard for either of them to contain their emotions.

"I went over to the school and there was a big pile of rubble," recalls Scott, who weeps as he delves back into the memory. "I went back to where they were digging the kids out and kept waiting. Finally the first responders told us that they had taped off the area, and we had to leave. I found a hot water tank sitting out behind the school, and I went and sat down on it. After a while, I saw them pull a little boy out."

Scott is now certain it was Nic that he saw pulled out of the debris on that day.

He recalls telling Chaplain Bunny Yekzaman, who came to weep with the McCabes, that "he's my only son."

During the next moments and days, they went through the

motions of decision-making, completely numb. No one could believe that Nicolas, at just eight years old, was gone.

Along with Nicolas, the child-like laughter disappeared from the McCabe's house.

"You should never have to prepare for your son's funeral," says Stacey, her voice thin with grief. "A child is full of life. Nicolas still had so much to give."

HURTING PARENTS FROM JOPLIN, MISSOURI AND MOORE, OKLAHOMA MEET.

Kari Carmona, now a single mother from Joplin, Missouri, and the four daughters she cares for understand much of what the McCabes have gone through.

Almost two years earlier to the day, on May 22, 2011, another EF5 tornado turned parts of Joplin, Mo., into hideous mountains of rubble. Kari's husband, Moises, and their daughter, Arriy, age eight, were also killed when their church building collapsed on top of them.

The four remaining girls remember the day as a typical spring afternoon, without an inkling that a tornado would later sweep through the town.

Kayla Carmona is Moises and Kari's oldest daughter, now 15. She recounts it this way: "When we got to the church that evening the pastor was in the back. He had the door wide open and was staring outside. When I looked past him, I saw the tornado in the parking lot."

Kayla shouted for everyone to take cover. She grabbed her two youngest sisters and ran for the nursery with the others, praying. There was screaming, and the lights went out. It seemed like only seconds before the building collapsed.

As the stunned and bloodied church members tried to crawl out of the rubble—pieces of the walls and ceiling, children's toys, chunks of plaster and wooden beams—they still couldn't comprehend the extent of the disaster.

But Moises and Arriy were gone, crushed by the walls and heavy ceiling beams that had fallen when part of the church building collapsed. When Kayla crawled out and found Arriy's limp body in a woman's arms, she still looked so lifelike that Kayla put a hand to her neck and could almost swear she felt a pulse.

Like the McCabes, life for Kari, Kayla, and the other Carmona daughters would never, ever be the same.

Everything they'd known for years vanished in a few gruesome moments.

And where was God?

Where was God when the walls crumbled around little Nicolas McCabe, and when the ceiling fell down on Arriy Carmona and her father? Why did other children walk away alive from Plaza Towers and Briarwood Elementary Schools while Nicolas and six others breathed their last? Why did the tornado veer straight into the church building in Joplin instead of cutting a swath of safety around the faithful group, where the Carmonas huddled praying? Where was God when the wind roared and the Enemy laughed, when God's precious children cried out to Him for deliverance?

Where was God when your sick mother took her last breath? When your beloved grandfather closed his eyes for the last time in the hospice room? Where was He when your friend's life was cut short in a car accident, when the grim-faced police officer knocked on your front door, when the obstetrician put down his stethoscope and said, "I'm sorry"?

Our losses aren't all front-page news tragedies like those in Joplin and Moore. But they're real, they hurt, and they're front-page in our own personal lives. It's likely that you will one day experience a loss that devastates you and leaves you in need of healing.

Our losses leave us empty, sore, like part of us is amputated forever. Whether it's someone we've lived with for years or it's the child still unborn that slips away before birth; a part of us is missing, gone, never to be replaced. Post-abortive women frequently need counseling when they come to the conclusion that the life they eliminated was precious and left an emotional hole in them.

Some grief counselors I spoke with not long ago said that even the loss of beloved pets can cause pain and loss that takes therapy to continue functioning without continual weeping and the desire to hide from the world.

What exactly is God doing when we're aching inside from the loss?

The loss of a loved one, especially a child, is likely the worst kind of disaster anyone can experience. It is every loving parent's worst nightmare; the endless anguish that never fades, no matter how much time passes.

Feelings betray themselves. A simple song or memory or shade of sunset can bring unexpected and sudden tears, and our emotions huddle in a strange no-man's land, always ready to slip out of our tight control. That's okay. That's how grief is.

Proverbs 14:13 sums it up succinctly: "Even in laughter the heart may ache, and rejoicing may end in grief."

However, may I suggest to you that this grief, while very real, is not the whole story. Your grief is not the totality of the life God has planned for you.

Even in the worst and most painful of circumstances, God has prepared blessings for you. God is always near, and He sometimes reserves His choice blessings for when we need them the most.

So far in this book, we've made a few passing references to Job, the most famous grieving sufferer in all history. But before we dig into the blessings that Scott and Stacey McCabe and the Carmonas have discovered, let's take a deeper look at what Job experienced, how it relates to our own pain, and how we can find blessings from God even in that pain.

As Satan, with God's permission, worked to destroy Job, the man of faith, at one point we read about the time Job learned from a messenger that all ten of his beautiful children had died without any warning, in a horrible disaster eerily similar to the ones that took Nicolas McCabe and Arriy and Moises Carmona.

While he was still speaking, yet another messenger came and said,

> "Your sons and daughters were feasting and drinking wine at the oldest brother's house, when suddenly a mighty wind swept in from the desert and struck the four corners of the house. It collapsed on them and they are dead, and I am the only one who has escaped to tell you!" (Job 1:18-19)

A careful reading of the story will reveal how painful Job's loss was to him. Clearly Job loved his children and longed for them to have a good relationship with the Lord. The family was also apparently close to one another, feasting regularly in one another's homes, which hints at the happy, united, loving family Job must have built with his wife. Not only that, but consider the escalating sequence of destruction in Satan's first attempts to goad Job into giving up his faith in God: the loss of the oxen, the sheep, the camels, and finally, the loss of Job's children; each successive loss seemed worse than the one before it, until the final blow.

Let's remember that Job was a righteous man who cared for his animals and for the needs of his workers. While we tend to think mainly of Job's pocketbook when Satan struck his livestock and workers, certainly his heart grieved at losing his faithful animals and workers who'd grown up in his house.

But the thing that cost him the most was the death of his beloved children. Immediately Job got up and tore his robe and shaved his head in an expression of deep grief.

And when Job looked back over his wonderful life, from the pit of deep despair and suffering, notice what he recalls in Job 29:4-5:

> Oh, for the days when I was in my prime,
> when God's intimate friendship blessed my house,
> when the Almighty was still with me
> and my children were around me...

In his darkest days, Job reveled in the memories of what he once had, which brings us to the first blessing we can glean as we grieve our losses.

1. OUR GRIEF CAN ALLOW US TO THANK GOD FOR HOW MUCH SOMEONE MEANT TO US.

It seems brutally unfair, but the more we love, the more pain we feel when that dear friend or relative or child is taken away. It is almost a natural law that loving relationships have the potential to bring as much sorrow as they do joy.

The anguish of watching a child die was described to Mary, the mother of Jesus, by aged Simeon as a deadly weapon: "and a sword will pierce your own soul, too" (Luke 2:35).

That description also fits how the hearts of the McCabes, Kari Carmona, and others who have lost a child must feel: stumbling along with a pierced soul, and a heart that is permanently broken in one tender place.

Loss shows you exactly how much you loved and were loved in return—and that love, as much as it hurts, was a blessing. *Is* a blessing.

Love is always a blessing.

We may not see it that way at first because it hurts so badly, but love changes us, matures us, softens us. It has a way of transforming us. Love, along with its life-changing beauty and power, is a blessing from God that remains with us even after our precious ones are gone.

For love, you see, was God's idea. To bless you. To bolster you in hard times. To reach out with human hands and show you a bit of God's own heart.

So what do we do when the pain of loss is so great that we can't feel the blessing of that deep, glorious love we enjoyed so much?

As a pastor, I've seen a couple of different scenarios play out many times over the past 22 years. For some, when they encounter the darkest kinds of hurt and loss, they run away from the Lord. The questions of "why" aren't so much questions wanting answers, but they tend to be angry accusations leveled at God. For others, rather than running *from* His arms, they run directly *to* Him.

For most people, though, there's ongoing tension between these two extremes. I find most people both run to and away from God, perhaps even repeatedly while grieving. Running into His arms, and also going through spells of deep anger and questioning. Loss has a clearly divisive effect. We tend to either get closer to the Lord or to push away from Him.

What is it that causes one person's experience of loss to propel them toward Jesus, and another to turn *away?* For me, this is one of the great mysteries of life.

What isn't a mystery is that in the fast paced blur of life, of school days and late nights and bill-paying and marital spats, we can forget what beautiful gifts from God our loved ones are.

Loss has a way of showing exactly how much people mean to us.

As his very first act as a grief-stricken survivor, Job chose to *praise* God who gives all things, and who had blessed him so greatly. His very first actions after the onslaught of bad news, and after tearing his robe, were these:

> At this, Job got up and tore his robe and shaved his head.
> Then he fell to the ground in worship and said:
>
> *"Naked I came from my mother's womb,*
> *and naked I will depart.*
> *The LORD gave and the LORD has taken away;*
> *may the name of the LORD be praised" (Job 1:20-22).*

After his initial expressions of sorrow, the shaving and the tearing, He *worshipped* God. His powerful words of gratefulness and praise, whispered by grieving believers for centuries, almost defy description.

This wounded man was able to give praise to the same God who had taken it all away. He recognized that the God who takes is also the God who gives, and he chose to give thanks.

Job was a normal man with normal emotions (which he fully expressed and lamented for the bulk of the text) but his first reaction was driven by choice. We can't always choose what we feel, but we can choose what we do with our emotions. We can choose to praise.

People who choose to worship God in the face of grief will tell you that praise is a powerful weapon against bitterness, rage, and depression.

However, as the next chapters of Job show, praising God in the midst of grief does not make everything okay. It does not remove the pain, and it does not bring back a lost loved one. It also does not take the place of true, honest conversation with God and friends, including the full spectrum of emotions from anger to numbness to sorrow and back again.

Remember, a cursory reading of the Psalms reveals that a third or more of all the psalms are laments in which the sufferer cries out to God authentically. At times, the psalmists cry out to God even in accusatory ways.

When I read the story of Job, the surprising part is how well Job initially took the devastating blows.

When I experience pain and suffering, I hope my own faith resembles that of Job's initial response rather than his wife's. But even in the darkest times of my brokenness, even when my pain turns into angry shouts and expressions directed at the Lord – even then, I can have confidence that my painful cries will be met with tenderness, mercy, compassion, and as much grace as I need. There will never be an end to the Lord crying with me and even wiping away my tears.

Even in the darkest times, when life beats us down, we can still choose one thing: To praise God no matter what. When we're broken with grief, we can get on our knees and worship our Master.

When our hearts are shattered, we can whisper these words of Job: "The Lord gives, and the Lord takes away, but blessed be the name of the Lord."

Remember, though, if you're comforting someone who's grieving, the choice to praise God belongs only to him or her. It cannot be forced. We dare not suggest it or push it or insinuate that the survivor is less than spiritual because he or she doesn't express the same faith in God that they used to (or that you think they should.)

Give grief stricken people time, and let God do His work on their aching hearts. He alone knows how to restore the broken. Any outside pressure to "be like Job" is likely to end in anger and hostility, or perhaps worse, a fake mask of piety that covers up what's actually happening inside.

If you're the one who's hurting, though, praising God in the storm can be a tender reaction to the terrible things happening around you.

When we think sorrow has stolen everything, it hasn't. We can still choose. We can still choose to praise our Creator. We can still choose to give thanks for the blessing of the one we loved so much. No person or situation can take away that right to pick our own attitudes and our words, no matter what we've been through.

When your world falls apart, choose to give thanks.

Then walk with the Savior through the next waves of emotion and grief, as they ripple through your heart for a lifetime.

We need to make sure and understand though, that choosing to praise God during times of loss doesn't take away our need to express our honest feelings openly, which is essential for any grief journey.

For even these are a blessing from God. The gentle way He created our emotions to require slow and deep healing; the tears He created to give voice to our unspoken thoughts, and the unfolding process of grief that never, ever leaves us the same way.

God could have created us like robots—mechanical, unfeeling, cold, to operate with loss the same as we do with digestion.

But He didn't. He made us feeling, weeping, remembering. The way He is. The way we really live life to the full. The way we truly love.

2. GRIEF, IN ITS FULL AND PAINFUL SPECTRUM, IS ACTUALLY A GREAT BLESSING FROM GOD.

Job certainly grieved and held nothing back.

Lest you picture Job as some kind of overly pious, super-spiritual type who only spouted platitudes and said "the right thing," think again. Check out these samplings that seem as if Job is even railing against the Lord throughout the book:

» He cursed the day of his birth and wished that he'd been still-born or never born at all (Job 3 and 10);

» He said his misery weighs more than the sand in the seas (6:3-4) and compared God's actions against him to poison and deadly arrows (6:5);

» He accused his friends of being morally deficient and of no help whatsoever (chapter 6);

» Job said he hates his life so much that he would prefer being strangled to death over actually living (chapter 7);

- » He felt like God was angry with him for some unknown reason, that God made Job his enemy, and that God was wreaking unfair vengeance on him when he was actually innocent (chapters 10 and 11);
- » Job said that evil men actually appeared to prosper and escape punishment, while the righteous suffered (chapter 21, 24);
- » He says that God just did what He wanted, regardless of how much it made Job suffer (chapter 23);
- » Job longed for the past, for the days when life was good (chapter 29) and compared how dreadful his life was (chapter 30);
- » Job lists all the righteous things he has done throughout his life and questions why they don't seem to matter to God (chapter 31).

So whatever your impressions of Job are, please don't assume he was an emotionless, over-righteous man who prayed stilted prayers and separated his heart and emotions from his faith.

No. Job was a real, flesh-and-blood, grieving man who'd lost almost everything he'd ever loved—and his emotions raged with little control. He lashed out at his friends, at the injustice of it all, and even at God, bitterly lamenting his fate. He wished for justice. He wanted to die. He even demanded an audience with God himself, which God gave him later in the book.

Initially, Job's friends were helpful and quiet, saying nothing for a week. But when they started opening their mouths, they were really damaging. Instead of allowing Job to openly express his feelings, they accused him of wrongdoing. They inaccurately suggested that the

God-ordained order of things wouldn't allow this much trouble to fall on an innocent man.

It sounds righteous enough. Job's friends just wanted to show how man, and not God, is at fault in matters of disaster, right? They insisted that Job's suffering was the result of Job's sin or unrighteousness. For them, tragedy was reserved for sinners and those who deserved God's judgment.

Job spoke loudly and bitterly against the idea that his suffering was caused by sin in his life. He complained that God had the power to deliver him, but He didn't; he lamented the unfairness of his plight, the injustice of evil men whom God seems to let go scot-free and unpunished, and the overwhelming power in these blows God struck him with.

"God did it!" Job seemed to scream. "God did it all, every single thing. And give me five minutes with him. I'll tell him exactly what I think about it."

While Job's friends tried to let God off the hook, Job put God squarely in the center and refused to allow any excuses or mincing of words.

The position of Job's friends might sound spiritual, protective of God, even, but at the end of the book of Job, God corrects this idea.

> After the Lord had said these things to Job, he said to Eliphaz the Temanite, "I am angry with you and your two friends, because ***you have not spoken the truth about me, as my servant Job has***. So now take seven bulls and seven rams and go to my servant Job and sacrifice a burnt offering for yourselves. My servant Job will pray for you, and I will accept his prayer and not deal with you according to your folly. You have not spoken the truth about me, as my servant Job has" (Job 42:7-8).

Wait, God was angry at... *Job's friends?* It's not just that they got their doctrine a little bit wrong. No, their attitudes and words were skewed enough to actually make God angry at them. So angry that God asked Job to offer sacrifices for them and pray for them, and only *then* would he accept their prayers and spare them punishment!

For those grieving, these are strong words!

God wants, more than anything, *to hear from you in authenticity.* Share with Him in your real words, your real heart. Don't put on a false religious front. God can handle your criticism and challenges. He is not afraid of your questions. He can still love you and heal your heart with everything that is in it.

Biblically, lamenting - or expressing deep grief which always includes asking painful questions, is one of the key ways that we can connect with God. I love the way Waltke and Houston describe lament:

> "Biblically, lament is a transition, like the Exodus, a tempted environment of murmurings and distrust, or a joyful anticipation of the Promised Land. As Oswald Bayer has observed: Systematic theology in general tends to refer to a happy ending all too hastily and fails to take seriously the fruitless disorientations of the journey in all its uncertainties. ***Joy is the last word, but lament may fill much of a Christian's earthly sufferings.*** Søren Kierkegaard, who reflected much upon Job, left his mark in a corner of Copenhagen's cathedral Vor Frue Kirke [its name] dedicated to Job and to all lamenters, in a creedal statement: We believe that God is great enough to harbor our little lives with all their grievances, and that he can lead us from darkness through to the other side.' Then through the semi-darkness, the eye can begin to see dimly pinned to a picture of a cross, the words of the apostle

> Peter: 'Cast all your anxiety upon him because he cares for you' (1 Pet 5:7)."[33]

"Joy is the last word, but sadness may fill much of a Christian's earthly sufferings."

After losing her daddy and her baby sister in the Joplin storm, young Kayla Carmona relates to the range of emotions from fury to bitterness and hurt.

"When the storm [in Joplin] hit, of course we were crying out to God," she recalls. "A few weeks later, I wasn't really interested in life anymore. I was done."

Like most grief survivors, Kayla didn't feel anything for a while.

By about the six month mark, she even told God, "I hate you. Why would you do this to Your children? Why would You hurt me so badly?" For almost the entire first year, after the death of her sister and father, Kayla says it was almost like God wasn't in her life at all.

In July after the tornado, Kayla was feeling all that emptiness, and she went to an outreach sponsored by the Salvation Army called the "Hope Station." They offered devotionals and recovery materials. Over time, people met at the *Hope Station*, shared their stories, and the recovery process slowly started for the Carmonas. Over time, Kayla and her now single mother Kari, started helping with other small recovery events. Kayla says, "That's when I started to understand hope, and that hope comes from Jesus."

But her feelings of faith and trust in God weren't restored overnight, and the memory of her loss is still incredibly hard. Significantly, God never did answer her question, "Why?"

Kayla thinks of those two painful, dark years as a long journey that

---

33 *The Psalms as a Christian's Lament: A Historical Commentary*, Bruce Waltke and James Houston (Grand Rapids, MI: Wm. B. Eerdmans Publishing Co.), 4.

at times seemed empty of meaning. But it wasn't without purpose. "I think that before the tornado I wasn't sold out completely to God," she says. "I was half-heartedly doing everything. I went to church. I was this good Christian girl, but I wasn't giving my all. I think that's what God has been wanting, for me to give my all."

Kari Carmona, Kayla's mom, has had a similarly hard journey. "I didn't plan on going back to church," she says. She describes the grief as being so tangible that she can literally feel the heaviness in her chest at times.

The questions of "why" never really ended, either, Kari says.

How long will it hurt? For a long time. Maybe even for a lifetime, appearing and reappearing throughout time and events, weaving its way in the shadows of the background. Sometimes coming sharply and unexpectedly to the forefront and making us hurt all over again, long after others might think we should be "over it" by now.

But even the dark moments can be healing, too, as all the colors, events, and memories swirl together into the healing pattern God has planned.

So if you're the one comforting a grieving friend, let them grieve.

Which is exactly where Job's friends failed. They consistently tried to push their own erroneous doctrine on him, to shame him into admitting guilt when there was none, and to hush up his emotional outbursts.

Initially, Job's friends got it right, when they sat with him in silence during Job's unspeakable grief. Job 2:11-13 records it this way:

> When Job's three friends, Eliphaz the Temanite, Bildad the Shuhite and Zophar the Naamathite, heard about all the troubles that had come upon him, they set out from their homes and met together by agreement to go

> and sympathize with him and comfort him. When they saw him from a distance, they could hardly recognize him; they began to weep aloud, and they tore their robes and sprinkled dust on their heads. Then they sat on the ground with him for seven days and seven nights. No one said a word to him, because they saw how great his suffering was.

For seven days they sat with him. They tore their own robes in sorrow and wept aloud, and stayed by his side in solidarity.

Until, one by one, each man decided to open his mouth and try to "correct" Job's way of thinking. That was the first mistake.

Here are some brief tips I've accumulated over the years for helping minister to grieving people:

• UNDERSTAND THERE'S NO NORMAL WAY TO GRIEVE.

Grieving generally involves extremes in emotions. It's important not to tell someone how he or she "should" feel. Don't judge or be critical. Leave your "Mr. Fixit" tendencies at home when you visit a grieving friend.

Many things contribute to how people expect us to grieve.

Every culture has emotional tools to deal with the pain of loss. Some have traditions of subdued quietness and only private tears. Others celebrate with jubilant noise and parties. But even with the great cultural variations on grieving, each person will be completely unique. Some will lean into the traditions they know and will find great comfort while others feel the need to do the opposite.

Our personalities, gifts, and temperaments impact our grieving.

Our moods, hormones, and how in touch we are with our emotions also vary greatly. Some want to be around people and talk non-stop, others want silence and solitude, and yet others will find solace in some form of creative arts.

It's tempting to encourage others to mourn in the same way that you yourself mourn, but resist that compulsion! God made each of us as individuals and the way we grieve will always be an expression of that beautiful uniqueness.

• AFFIRM THE SITUATION AND THEIR FEELINGS.

Let them feel comfortable crying in your presence. Don't rationalize or reason with the grieving person. Don't push back on what they say. Let him or her express their feelings freely. Don't minimize their feelings by saying, "I know exactly how you feel." Use affirming words like, "I'm so sorry this happened."

Using mirroring language can also be affirming. When they say, "It just hurts so bad," you can affirm them by repeating it. "I'm so sorry that this hurts you so bad." Repeating their words is an indicator that you "get it."

• DON'T TAKE THINGS PERSONALLY.

This time that your friend is grieving isn't about you. If things arise where your feelings are hurt, if they cancel dinner plans with you, if they say harsh things to you, you'll need to swallow your pride and deal with that as part of the process of helping someone. When we grieve, we ride a roller coaster of emotions. It's natural to take it out on whoever happens to be close.

• HELP THEM WITH PRACTICAL THINGS.

Clean the house, bring food, take calls for them, mow the yard, take them to lunch, go grocery shopping. Even the most mundane tasks can be difficult when someone is in pain.

Here's a practical note for you: the statement, "Call if I can do anything!" is meaningless. A grieving person will not call you, ever. Just look for things you can do to help, and do them. They may not even know what those things are.

• DON'T LET THEM BE ISOLATED.

Being alone is normal and necessary for most people in the grieving process for limited times. But social isolation is not good for anyone. This is where you encourage your friend and take them places with you.

• DON'T CARRY THE FULL WEIGHT OF SOMEONE'S RECOVERY.

Don't work harder at helping them than they work on it themselves, but if he or she will let you, do practical things for them like taking them out for dinner or to shop for groceries with you.

• WATCH FOR SIGNS OF PROBLEMS.

Weeks of isolation, talking about dying or suicide, substance abuse, not enjoying anything in life - these types of indicators, especially if it's after the first couple of months of grieving, are signs you should probably recommend professional help.

• ALWAYS TAKE TALK OF SUICIDE SERIOUSLY.

This is when it's time to take action. Get professional help for them right away. It's normal for any grieving person to think about death and dying. But if they mention wanting to die, or seem to focus on it, or mention suicide at all, ask them very directly, "Are you thinking about hurting yourself?"

At this stage, as a pastor, I tell them directly, "When you grieve and cry and are hurting, I can cry with you. But I need to know if you're thinking about suicide or hurting yourself. If that is the case, I'll have to make some calls right now."

Any time someone tells you they plan to hurt themselves, call 911 and start taking steps to intervene.

• SIT IN SILENCE AND LISTEN.

Many times grieving people want and need to tell their story repeatedly. This is a great help. Just listen to them, even if they've shared the same story already. They may talk about what happened, what the doctors said, the last conversation they had... just listen. The more silent we are, the less we can hurt them. Sometimes even the kindest things we can say, such as, "You're so strong" can prevent them from feeling free to be vulnerable and broken.

In short, with bereaved parents or friends, less is probably more.

Because they've already got all they can handle right now. They have more emotion than they have clear thought, and more questions than answers.

This brings me to a common question grieving parents often ask:

“Are my children in Heaven?” “Is my unborn baby with Jesus?” “Where is she now?”

Scott and Stacey McCabe were right when they said no one should have to bury a child. It’s not natural; it’s not right or normal. It feels so *wrong.*

Because it is.

We were not designed in Eden to have our children die, for babies to be stillborn or stop forming in the womb. For disease to ravage our once-healthy daughters and sons, or for drunk drivers and accidents to take their lives in a matter of minutes.

So what does God do with children who die before they are old enough to decide to follow Christ?

Let me point you to the Father who loves you, and uncover yet another hidden blessing: the compassionate, loving character of our God as revealed in Scripture

3. WE CAN TRUST GOD WITH OUR BABIES AND CHILDREN WHO HAVE PASSED AWAY.

As with other mysteries, the Bible says little about this, but what the Bible does say compels me to confidently believe that babies, children, and those handicapped and unable to cognitively choose to trust Christ, once swept out of this world, wake up in the arms of Jesus and our Heavenly Father.

Sam Storms, theologian and pastor from Oklahoma City, wrote a great overview of the various Christian responses to this topic in a 2006 blog post titled, “Are Those Who Die in Infancy Saved?” My views are not identical to Dr. Storm’s but his article helped me understand better how different Bible scholars approach the issue.

Without the Bible directly addressing the salvation of kids and infants, we must rely on clues we get from scripture. In addition to these hints, the greatest evidence we have for what God does with our little ones is found in what we do clearly know about God – His character.

God is good. He loves our children and they are safe in His arms.

Here are just a few reasons many Bible teachers suggest that children, infants, and the cognitively handicapped are saved by Jesus when they die, and that we'll see them again.

• ALL THOSE WITHOUT RECEIVING GENERAL REVELATION ARE "WITH EXCUSE."

Romans 1:19-20 says this:

> "For what can be known about God is plain to them because God has shown it to them. For his invisible attributes, namely, his eternal power and divine nature, have been clearly perceived, ever since the creation of the world, in the things that have been made. Therefore, they are without excuse."

These verses seem to say people are judged by their response to what they have seen and "clearly perceived" about God. Children and babies obviously aren't able to "clearly perceive" the things of God. In that case, they could be viewed as being ***with an excuse,*** as opposed to the adults who are ***without excuse*** because they know the truth.

• THEY HAVE NO KNOWLEDGE OF GOOD AND EVIL.

Hell is for the devil and his angels and those who willingly and voluntarily choose to follow them by rejecting Christ. Babies and children do not have a full knowledge of sin and wickedness, and neither do they have the mental capacity to rationalize their behavior and "choose" to follow Satan or to reject Christ. They simply respond to their environment and their caretakers, slowly growing in knowledge and understanding, until a later date at which they might be considered "accountable" or "responsible" for their own actions and choices.

Deuteronomy 1:39 even specifically says that kids, "do not yet know good from bad."

• THE BIBLE IMPLIES THAT DAVID'S BABY WENT TO HEAVEN.

In 2 Samuel 12:15-23, we read a tragic story about David losing his firstborn son. After David's time of fasting and mourning, he made a statement relevant to our discussion here. David said in verse 23, "But now that he is dead, why should I go on fasting? Can I bring him back again? *I will go to him, but he will not return to me.*"

• WE'RE TO BE JUDGED BASED ON OUR DEEDS.

"For we must all appear before the judgment seat of Christ, so that each of us may receive what is due us for the things done while in the body, whether good or bad." This teaching found in 2 Corinthians 5:10 seems to say we're judged according to our actual deeds.

Are infants able to knowingly reject God and choose to sin? No. We don't see any example in Scripture of people being judged by God as unrighteous outside of willingly rejecting Him.

• WE HAVE A FEW EXAMPLES OF INFANTS KNOWING GOD EVEN IN THE WOMB.

Regardless of parentage, God adores, chooses, and delights in His innocent little ones. In fact, God's closeness to children, including unborn children in the womb, is recorded multiple times in Scripture.

Some examples are : "...from my mother's womb you have been my God" (Psalm 22:10); "From birth I have relied on you; you brought me forth from my mother's womb" (Psalm 71:6); "Listen to me, O house of Jacob... you whom I have upheld since you were conceived, and have carried since your birth" (Isaiah 46:3). In Luke 1 John the Baptizer was recorded as being "filled with the Spirit" even from birth—and having a spiritual call on his life before he was born.

Consider God's tender closeness to this infant in Psalm 139:13-16: "For you created my inmost being; you knit me together in my mother's womb. My frame was not hidden from you when I was made in the secret place. When I was woven together in the depths of the earth, your eyes saw my unformed body. All the days ordained for me were written in your book before one of them came to be."

• WE CAN TRUST WHAT WE KNOW ABOUT THE CHARACTER OF GOD.

Not only did Jesus fiercely protect children, but they are always pictured in Scripture as close to God's heart, and close to the kingdom of Heaven, watched constantly by angels who stand in the presence of God (Matthew 18:10). Kids first recognized Jesus' authority and kingship in Matthew 21 as they cried out to him in the streets, "Hosanna to the Son of David!"

As Jesus looked at those children and loved them, He said to the indignant scoffers that complained: "Have you never read, 'From the lips of children and infants, you, Lord, have called forth your praise?'" He was, quoting Psalm 8:2, which had been penned centuries earlier.

Did you catch that? Read it again.

"From the lips of children." Yes, we can picture that. We can imagine older children recognizing Jesus' majesty and loving heart and voicing their happy adoration. But after that, the verse says, "*...and infants*." How can an infant praise God? "Infants" can't even talk, much less make spiritually mature statements.

Is it possible that just by "being" who they are – that these beautiful children and infants—born and unborn—cry out daily their praise to God? That their very attitudes reflect their "instincts" to praise their Creator? When Wordsworth the poet wrote that "Heaven lies about us in our infancy,"[34] he spoke out loud what most of us feel when we look at babies. They are beautifully innocent beings that seem almost too otherworldly and perfect for this broken, sinful, fallen earth. They belong in Heaven. They belong with their Maker.

Some of them have been taken to Heaven, to be with their loving God.

When our children pass away at a young age, be assured that the God who formed them in the womb, who loves them, and who has ordained all of their days on earth is tenderly caring for them in their heavenly home, where they will never grow old, never feel pain, and

---

34 *Famous Lines: A Columbia Dictionary of Familiar Quotations*, Robert Andrews (New York: Columbia University Press), 70.

never cry over our bad parenting mistakes.

A home where they're anxiously waiting for you, like a child with his nose pressed to the glass of the toy store. Scott and Stacey McCabe, and Kari Carmona, and Rhett and Misty Burnett, plus so many others who have lost children wait with great anticipation for the day they will be reunited with their precious little ones.

Before we move on to the next principle, I want to mention a couple more things. It's common for parents to say that they have had visions or dreams that testify to how safe and happy their kids are in heavenly arms. It would be hard to discredit so many who experience this. Such dreams aren't really addressed in scripture, so we can't base our faith on them, but it's comforting to hear the detailed dreams that some believing friends have experienced; dreams where they see their children's or siblings' radiant faces, see them sitting in the throne room or playing in beautiful fields with Jesus and angels, and sometimes even talk with them.

Since God deeply loves His children—His little ones and his grown ones—it's not unrealistic that He would use dreams, visions, and other supernatural means to impart comfort to desperately grieving hearts.

But above all else, we can trust that our children and babies are safe *because we know the heart of God*. We know the One who made them, who formed them in the womb, and who held their tiny hands as they took their last breath. And we know the tender shepherd who gathers them to himself with joy. "He tends his flock like a shepherd: *He gathers the lambs in his arms and carries them close to his heart*; he gently leads those that have young" (Isaiah 40:11).

Jesus cares for those of you who have lost children, friends. Isaiah says He "gently leads" those that have young. He is gentle with your grief, and tender with your crushing loss.

Most of us will never discover how deep and precious these truths are until we walk through the valley of the shadow of death ourselves, and find God's comforting presence walking with us, beside us, with His arms around us. If we can only open our grieving hearts long enough to see it, and reach out for the hope He offers.

Remember, God knows how it feels to lose a child, too—a Son. His only Son. A perfect Son who was stripped, beaten, whipped, and nailed to a wooden cross on our behalf. He knows what you have been through. He watched His "beloved Son, in whom [He was] well pleased" grow from a helpless baby to a grown man who touched lepers and prayed forgiveness for those who murdered him.

Then He watched his Son die.

Do we ever think about how God grieved, wept, and cried out in anguish as Jesus breathed his last? He knows, friends. He leads you gently.

He has gathered those precious lambs in his arms—the littlest ones, the weakest ones —holding them close to his heart, waiting to enfold you both in his loving embrace.

And as you walk toward that moment, remember this:

4. DARK DAYS BRING LONELINESS, BUT THE DARKNESS CAN GIVE WAY TO TRANSFORMATION.

During the darkest and hardest of days, people who experience loss will almost always, without exception, admit how alone they felt during that dark period. We have a hard time recognizing God's presence when we're drowning in raw emotions. It doesn't feel like He's answering our prayers or that He's even there. During loss, it may even feel as if God is an enemy.

It's only when the gloomy clouds begin to lift a little that we realize something has changed. We have changed. We are new people now; we live in a "new normal" that will never be quite like the old life we used to have.

PAIN GIVES US A LONGING FOR ETERNITY.

"In November 2012, we found out we were expecting, and we were very excited because we had been trying," says Shawna Sisney, 32, a wife and homeschooling mom in Oklahoma City.

All of that changed at the eleven-and-a-half week mark, when Shawna discovered she had lost their baby. In what is commonly known as a "missed miscarriage," their precious baby had already slipped into eternity weeks before, without a single symptom, and they had not even realized it.

"Our joy quickly turned to tears," recalls Shawna. "I was mad at God. 'How could He let this happen? Why did we have to go four more weeks getting more attached to our baby that had already been taken into Heaven?"

Shawna didn't feel like it, but she was compelled to start playing worship music, and even dancing to the songs with her six year old son, Caleb.

"It turned my heart around," she says. "I started to seek God more and draw closer to Him. I understood that Christ knew the pain I felt because He felt that pain when He died on the cross for me. And I knew He was the only one that could heal my heart because He's the One who conquered sin and death."

Not long after, Shawna and her husband, Ben found out they were pregnant with another baby, Eliana Hope, the sister Caleb wanted so badly.

"I was able to walk in faith and not fear," says Shawna. "I continued to thank God that He had a plan for this baby—'a plan to prosper it and not to harm it, a plan to give it a hope and a future'(Jeremiah 29:11). We're so excited. I can't wait until she comes. I think about it all the time.

"The miscarriage has given us all an eternal perspective. It's only when we run to God that we can find the healing, comfort, and peace that surpasses all understanding."

An eternal perspective: a look at life from a different view. A heavenly one. This new perspective will be with them for the rest of their days.

GRIEF MAKES US MORE AWARE OF SIMPLE JOYS.

Chase and Alise Newby also experienced loss when their house was destroyed in the 2013 tornado. We think of grief as mostly losing someone we love, but anytime something irreplaceable escapes us, part of our heart is torn.

Alise, this 30 year old mom from Moore, describes her loss this way:

"When I got out of the shelter I was panicking, in shock to find Liam, our oldest son in the school rubble. When I found he was okay, we headed back to our house. We found the garage, the boy's room, the playroom, the office, and the roof had all gone."

Their home was two houses away from being entirely scraped off the slab by the harsh winds.

In the middle of all of the mess of the front yard, Alise saw something that struck her as funny, which gave her a moment of joy, and that will stay with her for the rest of the life.

All morning before the tornado, she had worked to remodel their bathroom, cutting trim by hand with a handsaw, leaving blisters and frustration. "If only I had a table saw, Lord!" she said several times. After finding her son, Liam, Alise returned to the fresh debris pile they used to call home.

As she walked up to the yard, right in front was a table saw.

For outsiders, this experience may seem unimportant. But in that moment, Alise was able to laugh about her earlier prayer; a moment of levity during the trial. A bit of joy in the middle of tragedy. She felt that God had spoken to her personally.

"I had a rush of relief and a sense that God was telling me, 'Chin up! I'm with you.' I needed that moment of joy. It gave me the peace I needed to hold myself together," she says.

This was the first of many personal and intimate blessings Chase and Alise experienced as they recovered from the disaster and mourned the loss of pictures, keepsakes, and memories.

From now on, finding and appreciating those small moments of joy will be simpler for this precious family. God has changed the way they view the world.

TRAGIC LOSS CAN BRING US CLOSER TO JESUS.

Scott and Stacey McCabe attest to God's work in their lives even during the darkest times of losing eight year old Nicolas.

"When we were told that Nicolas had died, that he was not coming home," Stacey says, "I knew he was in Heaven. Where was God? He was there. He had his protective hand over those seven children. He scooped them up. When that wall fell on them, God was there to take them away. They woke up and rejoiced because they were in Heaven."

Nicolas' death was a turning point that ushered in a time of spiritual strengthening and closeness to God in a way that Stacey had never known. Although she has believed the gospel for many years, things are different for her spiritually now. She has gone from believing to a place of action and sharing Christ's love with others.

As she has grown closer to the Lord, and an eternal perspective, she is convinced that her spiritual enemy wants to use this tragedy to destroy her faith.

"Shortly after Nicolas died, I had a terrible dream. I know it was the work of the devil," she recalls. "It had to be from the pits of hell. I saw that wall falling on Nicolas. That's where the dream stopped. But that's not where it was supposed to stop. Satan didn't show me the best part – that Nicolas was there, touched by God, and how he had gone straight home to Him. All Satan showed me was the hurtful parts."

Stacy's response is substantial, especially in the face of her pain: "I laughed at Satan and said, 'But you forgot something. You forgot to show me the rest of it.'"

Scott also experienced life change after Nicolas' death brought him what he never had before: baptism and salvation in Jesus Christ. First he heard testimonies from Kari and Kayla Carmona, and their hope and faith ignited something empty inside of him, as well as meeting with other believers who had suffered similar losses.

"Rhett Burnett was telling me that we are in a club," says Scott. "We buried our children. He lost a seven-year-old little girl to cancer, and he's offered to help me. I've got his card in my pocket. But when I went to church the first day and I saw he was an assistant pastor there, that made me want to go even more."

From that first day, Scott became increasingly interested in finding out about the Jesus that he knew only as a "friend," but not yet a "Savior." However, the more he learned about Jesus, the more he learned about everything in his life, including one of his main purposes for living.

Now, Scott says, he realizes that God wants to be a father to *him*.

"I love Him," says Scott. "With all my heart, even though my heart is broken. Because He's the healer."

Scott and Stacey are finding out that Nicolas' death is anything but the end.

I love hearing Scott talk about how he first decided to make Jesus the Lord of his life. At the end of a church service, we had a prayer time. I asked everyone to bow their heads and close their eyes. Then I said, "If any of you are interested in making Jesus the new Lord, or manager of your life, raise your hand and make eye contact with me." I'll never forget when my eyes met Scott's teary and decisive eyes.

"The door opened," says Scott. "Like, 'Come on in, Holy Spirit!'"

"I want to have a closer relationship with the Lord," he says. "My son didn't get the chance because we didn't give that to him. We didn't take him to church. Now God's giving *me* the chance. I'm still a work in progress."

Scott McCabe was baptized on his birthday, in a t-shirt that reminded him of Nicolas, not long after he made that profession of faith in church.

And so began Scott's new life in Christ. He uses a beginner's Bible to help him find the right passages, and he goes to small group meetings and church with Stacey. Mostly, he prays, out loud and simply, like a man talking to a friend.

"I'll go out there in the driveway, and I'll pace back and forth, and ask, 'What do you want me to do, God?' You know. Just a normal conversation like I'm talking to someone at work."

BROKENNESS GIVES US MINISTRY OPPORTUNITIES.

After the Joplin tornado, Kari and Kayla Carmona's story continued when they began ministering to the hurting in Moore; something they'd never even imagined.

Inspired by the Carmona's desire to travel (and eventually move) to Moore to minister to the hurting, a group of survivors from the Moore tornado traveled to Brookport, Illinois to minister to tornado survivors there, just months after the Moore storm, while wreckage was still on the ground. Kayla shared her testimony and volunteered among the hurting yet again. While there, she met a boy about her age who had lost his dad.

"I got to sit down and talk with him a little," Kayla recalls. "That's when I began to realize that *it's really not about me*. I just need to look around at what God's doing in me because of the Joplin tornado."

So Kayla, her mom Kari, and her three younger sisters Mari, Savannah, and Adrie spend much of their lives reaching out to other hurting people. Why? Because of what the Lord has done for them and also because they believe it helps continue the legacy of their dad and hero, Moises Carmona.

It was well after the Joplin storm that Kayla came to appreciate her father's love for others, and more specifically his heroism in his last moments.

Immediately after the storm, all Kayla knew was that her dad was struggling to breathe. She heard him grunting under part of the building. It wasn't until much later that the pastor explained how Moises, Kayla's dad, was holding part of the building so it wouldn't crush others who were trying to get out. When everyone was out, there was no way for him to also escape.

His sacrificial and gentle spirit is what encourages the Carmonas to continue making a difference in the lives of others.

Kayla says that knowing her dad would be proud of her brings her great motivation. Kari regularly reminds Kayla of the times she reflects her dad's gentleness. "When I say something kind to my sister, when I'm just sharing my smile, I feel that's something he would have done."

There's always a bigger picture. God is always transforming us.

HOW GRIEVING TRANSFORMED THE MOST FAMOUS SUFFERER IN HISTORY!

Job must have thought that his story ended when Satan stopped troubling him with painful boils and loss of livestock and rejection by his former friends. He may have thought the story was over when his wealth was restored to double. After all, that's where the biblical narrative ends.

The story of Job—the triumph of faith in the darkest of moments —still gives us hope when we're suffering even thousands of years later. Job is the book of the Bible that people use when they want to wrap their minds around the idea of grief, what to do with it, and how to keep their faith when all around them seems lost. It is Job we look to when life makes no sense. When suffering seems to come out of nowhere we need an "eternal perspective."

Part of me would like to say, "Look! See how God used Job to help all of us because of what God allowed Job to endure?" While that statement would be accurate, that idea would have been hardly comforting for Job as he experienced his tragedies. In scripture, we see how his faith was tested, wrecked, salvaged, repaired, and then restored.

Job held tight to God until God answered, showing up right there in the clouds and the lightning, speaking through the thunder, and shattering the deafening silence that Job probably assumed would last forever.

"Listen!" says the voice in Job 37 and 38. *"Listen to the roar of his voice, to the rumbling that comes from his mouth. He unlashes his lightning beneath the whole heaven and sends it to the ends of the earth. After that comes the sound of his roar; he thunders with majestic voice."*

Thunder and lightning in the voice of God.

"God's voice thunders in marvelous ways; He does great things beyond our understanding."

God's presence was in the rumbling, the churning, and the darkness of boiling clouds.

"Then the Lord spoke to Job out of the storm..."

God, the maker of the universe, spoke to Job through the storm.

Not before the storm, and not after it, but *during the storm itself,* answering Job from a whirlwind.

God spoke to Job in a whirlwind, the same type of damaging winds that took Job's children.

The same kind of wind that broke Job's heart and crushed his dreams.

Only this time God used the storm to speak to Job's heart, and to shift Job's questions and emotions into heavenly perspective. A perspective and a Divine encounter that would leave Job irrevocably changed. A perspective that transformed Job's heart.

Many of us want an audience with God, yet few of us are willing to pay the price Job paid for such a privilege, for such an encounter with

God, for such transformation within His own heart. What did Job's experience require before he experienced God in the deepest way? It required nothing less than a crawl through the darkest and wildest of storms.

Those who are battered the hardest by life's storms are often granted an unparalleled closeness to the Divine that onlookers can only wonder about.

In all of these deeply personal situations of loss and grief—the stories of the McCabes, Carmonas, Shawna Sisney, and Alise, and even Job's story—there is something we notice only by seeing the entire aching narrative from beginning to end: *God was, and is, deeply at work constructing something beautiful in each of them.*

The difficulty is seeing His work through the pain, while we are still in deep pain, without the rich benefit of hindsight. It's much easier to look back after weeks, months, or years, and see where God was working.

5. LET GRIEF AND LOSS REMIND US OF OUR ULTIMATE REALITY.

Over the past several years, I've spent a good bit of time reflecting on pain, suffering, grief, and on how different people respond to it. Why is it that some face problems as if there is no hope and others face them with steely determination to overcome and live well through the suffering even in the midst of the great darkness?

I'm convinced that this depends on the degree to which the griever keeps the reality of Heaven, the final home for Christ followers, in front of them.

Why does it matter so much that we keep our eyes fixed on the reality of Heaven as followers of Christ?

If we keep a clear view of Heaven and eternity, we won't see death as the ultimate tragedy and continuing to live as our ultimate achievement. It's when we see survival as our end goal that we tend to get really broken. Unless Jesus comes back, everyone living now will eventually die. If surviving this life is my goal, I'm guaranteed to fail.

But in Christ, death can be a celebration; a homecoming for the one who loves Jesus, and the joy and anticipation of a glorious reunion together in Heaven.

If we trust in the Christ who died for us and prepared a place for us in Heaven, we can have confidence that such a great existence will be ours. Like the Carmonas with Moises and Arriy, or the McCabes and Nicolas, we will walk together in gloriously restored bodies that will never age and grow old, and the imperfect love you shared on earth will only be magnified into exhilarating joy that exceeds everything you've ever known. You will have all eternity to be together with loved ones, gloriously worshipping Christ in a newly created world that glitters with perfection.

Heaven, according to the book of Revelation, is a mind-boggling swirl of blinding light, color, praise, and thundering voices. There is plenty going on; John describes strange angelic creatures crying out and books opening and lightning flashing. A sword flashes from the mouth of a dazzling Christ, and trumpets blast. A sparkling river runs through the city, and a tree unfurls special leaves for the "healing of the nations."

C.S. Lewis, the master of metaphors paints some great pictures of time, space, and the ultimate reality. Imagine that all of life is a book, he says. God is the author, and we're part of the story. The book represents all we know of time and space. It's our "reality." But now consider that the author lives completely outside of this reality in another dimension. He lives beyond us.

Or imagine a painting, and in the same way, we're painted into this portrait, but the canvas and two dimensional painting limits our reality. For the painter, though, he's so far beyond that reality.

Such is the nature of eternity. Eternity isn't just a length of time (quantitative) it's also an entirely different existence (qualitative.)

Another common pastoral explanation of eternity is to imagine a rope running from where you are now. Imagine it runs from your feet out the door, down the block, across town, through your state. Now imagine it goes all the way around the world multiple times. Now look down at your feet on the rope. There's a tiny scratch on it. That scratch represents all of time. The rope represents eternity in heaven.

This is why Dr. Sam Storms says, "The only ultimately and eternally safe place to be is in the arms of our heavenly Father from which no tornado or earthquake or tsunami or cancer or car wreck can ever snatch or wrench us free."[35]

Consider how Paul beautifully wrote about our otherworldly future existence in Christ in Romans 8:8, 20-2

> I consider that our present sufferings are not worth comparing with the glory that will be revealed in us. For the creation was subjected to frustration, not by its own choice, but by the will of the one who subjected it, in hope that the creation itself will be liberated from its bondage to decay and ***brought into the freedom and glory of the children of God***.

That is an incredible reality. Imagine how different life can be when I lean into the reality that one day everything will be changed.

---

35 "Tornadoes, Tsunamis, and the Mystery of Suffering and Sovereignty" in Enjoying God at samstorms.com, May 20, 2013 (http://www.samstorms.com/enjoying-god-blog/post/tornadoes--tsunamis--and-the-mystery-of-suffering-and-sovereignty, accessed July 18, 2015).

CONSIDER SOME OF THE PAINS IN THIS WORLD:

» **Life storms** – disappointment, financial, relational

» **Natural disasters** – destroying lives, property

» **Injustices –** oppression, broken systems that harm people

» **Illness and disability**

» **Sin, addictions, baggage, and brokenness**

» **Any other horror or tragedy our minds can conceive.**

Now dear friend, consider this. There will be a time, when every single wrong will be made right. Every injustice will be corrected. Every broken body will be healed. Every tragedy corrected. The Bible says "every tear will be wiped away." Take a look at a quick glimpse of how the book of Revelation describes this:

> "I saw the Holy City, the new Jerusalem, coming down out of heaven from God, prepared as a bride beautifully dressed for her husband. And I heard a loud voice from the throne saying, "Look! God's dwelling place is now among the people, and he will dwell with them. They will be his people, and God himself will be with them and be their God. 'He will wipe every tear from their eyes. There will be no more death' or mourning or crying or pain, for the old order of things has passed away" (Revelation 21:2-5).

Just imagine, one day the pains of this life will be no more!

Some people propose that the way to make it through life, to overcome, to stay on top of the circumstance, is through positive thinking. But this won't entirely solve our problem. I especially like the way author John Ortberg puts it, "The key is not positive thinking, it's eschatological thinking." The term eschatological refers to the end of the world and time itself. When time is no more![36]

You see, for a follower of Christ, the end of the book has already been written, and it is a happy ending.

This reality indicates that all of our suffering is temporary. Is it worth the suffering in order to experience perfect joy and the presence of God forever? C.S. Lewis answers this way, "They say of some temporal suffering, 'No future bliss can make up for it,' not knowing that Heaven, once attained, will work backwards and even turn that agony into a glory."[37]

Given this particular understanding, knowing what the future holds for those who suffer and are in Christ, is it possible that pain is actually a gift? Perhaps pain helps us to see what is slowly but definitely happening to this world. Maybe pain causes us to long for a different reality; a permanent reality. Pain and suffering help us to see the brokenness of our world causing us to long for the day when we're returned to our original state of joy.

When this world ends, we who call him "Father" will live there, in Heaven, forever, never again knowing pain or tears or death.

---

36 *The Life You've Always Wanted*, John Ortberg (Grand Rapids: Zondervan, 2002), 73.

37 *The Great Divorce*, C.S. Lewis (New York: HarpersCollins, 1946), 69.

This is the reason when we preach at funerals, one of the most common passages for comfort is 1 Corinthians 15:51-58. This section of God's word deals with how our bodies will be changed at the point that Jesus returns to the earth, to take His followers to live with Him forever.

The verses explain how those who die here and now will have their physical bodies raised back to life, put back together, and the souls that have passed on will be reunited with their bodies. Then those who are still living will be "changed" in an instant. Our bodies will change from being mortal to immortal. Our bodies will be perfect and they will no longer age or breakdown.

From this, we can infer that we'll recognize one another. And we'll certainly have community, love, relationships, joy, and all the good things our hearts long for. In a sense, at that point, we will be "restored" to how things were meant to be in the beginning. Perfect, unhindered joy and relationship with God and each other, not broken by sin, aging or the effects of time and suffering.

"Where, O death, is your victory?
Where, O death is your sting?" (1 Corinthians 15:55)

This "new-to-us" state of being won't actually be new at all! It's our ultimate reality. I love how Brennan Manning, a poet, priest, author, and speaker writes about this in his book, *Ragamuffin Gospel*:

> "What is the nature of Ultimate Reality? Jesus responds that the Really Real is generous, forgiving, saving love. In the end, will life triumph over death? With unshakable confidence, Jesus answers, 'The Kingdom of My Father cannot be overcome, even by death. In the end everything

> will be all right. Nothing can harm you permanently; no loss is lasting, no defeat more than transitory, no disappointment is conclusive. Suffering, failure, loneliness, sorrow, discouragement, and death will be part of your journey, but the Kingdom of God will conquer all these horrors. No evil can resist grace forever.'"[38]

Heaven is in fact, what we were made for. It is our ultimate reality. For a lover of Jesus, death is not an ending, it's a beginning.

How is it then, that we can be united with Christ in life and also in death?

Dear Lord Jesus, please help us to stare death in the face, acknowledge its ugliness, but still walk in faith. Help us to develop the faith of Job by seeing our losses but saying with confidence, "The Lord gives, the Lord takes away. Blessed be the name of the Lord." Please Lord, for any readers experiencing grief and loss, help them to walk through it like Scott and Stacey McCabe, open about the pain that has cut them like a sword from head to heart, but still able to praise You. ~ Amen

Dearest reader, there's hope for *you*.

If you're reading this, you can listen to Moses and the Prophets, to Jesus Christ the Messiah they prophesied about for centuries, and reach out in faith for salvation in Him.

This entire book has been about pain and suffering and how to find God in it.

The reality is this: we can't find God at all *except* for finding Him in pain and suffering. I'm not referring to our own human suffering. I'm

---

38 Brennan Manning, *Ragamuffin Gospel* (Portland: Multnomah, 2005) 199-200.

referring to the suffering of Christ.

During life's storm, God can be found in the same place He was found during His own Son's tragic death. Weeping. Loving. Caring. Planning to help us become more like Christ. Drawing us to Him.

Question: Why doesn't God do something about our suffering?

Answer: He did. He came to earth, clothed in human flesh and joined us in our suffering.

This is one of the primary concepts that separates Christianity from every other faith, every other world religion, every other worldview, every other philosophy for life; That God Himself, in the form of Jesus the Son, came to earth and participated in our suffering with us. He dove right into it.

American philosopher Nicholas Wolterstorff says this: "It is said of God that no one can behold His face and live. I always thought this meant that no one could see His splendor and live. A friend said perhaps it means that no one could see His sorrow and live. Or perhaps His sorrow is His splendor."[39]

That's a great way to explain it. The splendor of Jesus is that He willingly allowed his body to be tortured, brutalized, and murdered on the cross for the sins of all mankind. Jesus gave His all. Himself. His very flesh. To pay the price for our sins and to set the world on a path towards what would eventually be the perfecting of everything we know.

Because He died and rose again, we can live forever!

All that remains is to call out to Him in sincere brokenness. Acknowledge that before Him, I'm unworthy, I'm unfit. Then ask Him to be the Lord, or "Manager," of my life. When you accept Jesus as Lord,

---

39 *Lament for a Son*, Nicholas Wolterstorff, (Grand Rapids: Eerdmans, 1987), 81.

God makes you into a new person, what John 3 refers to as being "born again."

Heaven is glorious! Our existence will be remade into something far more beautiful than we can possibly imagine.

We can be certain, from the short conversation that Jesus had in Luke 23 that anyone who truly believes in Jesus can be saved, even if they're only moments away from death:

> One of the criminals who hung there hurled insults at (Jesus)... But the other criminal rebuked him. "Don't you fear God," he said, "since you are under the same sentence? We are punished justly, for we are getting what our deeds deserve. But this man has done nothing wrong." Then he said, "Jesus, remember me when you come into your kingdom." Jesus answered him, "Truly I tell you, today you will be with me in paradise" (Luke 23:39-43).

Right there, in two short sentences, a penitent criminal found salvation in Jesus Christ before he breathed his last. No rituals, no ceremony, no anything. Nothing except pure faith in Jesus Christ, and the realization that he had sinned against God.

Heaven was made for us. Remember, we are eternal beings!

Be encouraged, lover of God! You can trust God's mercy, His goodness, His love, justice, and righteousness. His goodness goes far beyond even our capacity to understand.

In your grief, run to His arms! In your pain, call out to Him!

Lie at His feet and offer as a sacrifice to Him all your concerns about your eternity as well as the eternity of your loved ones. Your Father in Heaven loves you and your family members more than you yourself love them.

If you don't know Him, please make today the day, and be sure of your eternity with Him. If you do know Him, celebrate in all He's done for us!

To hear more about Shawna Sisney's and Chase Newby's stories use the QR code below or go to www.WhereWasGod.com/book.

8

WHERE WAS GOD?

DURING LIFE'S STORMS, GOD IS ALWAYS NEAR

Where can I go from your Spirit?
Where can I flee from your presence?
If I go up to the heavens, you are there;
if I make my bed in the depths, you are there.
If I rise on the wings of the dawn,
if I settle on the far side of the sea,
even there your hand will guide me,
your right hand will hold me fast.
If I say, "Surely the darkness will hide me

and the light become night around me,"
even the darkness will not be dark to you;
the night will shine like the day,
for darkness is as light to you.

- Psalm 139:7-12 -

What kind of storm have you experienced? What are you going through right now? Perhaps it's not a natural disaster. Maybe you're going through a dark stormy night of family relational stress. The torrential winds and rains of financial tragedy. Tumultuous emotions due to illness and disability. Perhaps it's simply a lack of inner peace. When you're quiet and alone, the storm rages within you. Maybe it's most chaotic when it's quiet. Have you ever wondered, where is God in this storm?

When Chrysty and I came out of our storm shelter after the 2013 tornado, we found out, to our great relief, that our home hadn't been hit. It was still raining terribly, but I managed to get sporadic internet to my computer to see what was happening all over the city. A horrifying image burned into my mind: an aerial view of Briarwood Elementary as kids were crawling out of the wreckage.

The tornado completely destroyed two schools, Plaza Towers and Briarwood Elementary Schools. And Highland East Junior High took a direct hit so that much of it had to be rebuilt. I remember the sick feeling I had, with my own kids still at school. Had their schools been hit too? We also had friends and church kids at each of the three schools. Were they okay?

This is where Dr. Shelley McMillan, principal at Briarwood Elementary, comes in.

The night before the tragedy, Shelley was praying about the

weather. Weather forecasters predicted heavy thunder and rain, and the storm reports sounded ominous. Already a tornado veteran, Shelly had survived another EF5 tornado in Moore in 1999 by huddling in her bathtub with a mattress over her head. But facing a school full of children in the path of a deadly twister was a different matter.

"Dear Lord, this can't happen tomorrow. It can't happen again," she said the night before. But with her contagious positivity, Shelley pushed it aside proclaiming, "Tomorrow's going to be a great day!"

Besides that, really bad weather__if it materializes at all__ generally happens later in the afternoon, well after school is out. Living in "Tornado Alley" is like that. Storms and twisters can pop up in the spring time when conditions are right, generally in the evenings, and vanish in a few minutes, or leave overturned trees in their wake. Seldom do they cause significant damage in populated areas.

Still, for Shelley and her assistant principal, Jennifer Mankins, the possibility of a tornado was unsettling. But the skies were sunny, clear and bright for most of the day.

"We had our assembly as usual," Shelley recalls. "Everything was normal. We even had recess."

Then rain and hail suddenly began to pour. Parents started calling the school, and Shelley decided to do tornado drills just to be safe. In the afternoon, Shelley got a single email saying evening events were canceled. Nothing more. Tornado sirens went on, then off, then on again in an eerie fashion, and Shelley recalls walking to the back of the school and looking out over the fields.

There it was—a gigantic black twister, headed right for the school.

"I don't remember being afraid," recalls Shelley. "I went into 'what to do next' mode. After all, I'd done this before, and I could do it again. I went down the list, making sure the kids were in their places."

Shelley and Jennifer went from room to room making sure teachers and staff were making preparations. She describes how God gave her an inexplicable calm in her spirit. "I felt strongly that God told me no one was going to die here," she says. "Even when it got scary, I had that peace."

Shelley barely had time to squeeze into a safe spot with her secretaries when the tornado hit the building, tearing the roof off right over their heads. As bits of roof and sky and debris swirled above them, slow motion-like, Shelly remembers desperately trying to text her husband.

As Murphy's Law would have it, she couldn't find the "o" on her cell phone, so her texts read, "*I live you! I live you!*"

After the tornado roared past, Briarwood Elementary School ended up sprawled in a heap of debris, the building completely destroyed. Several teachers lay buried under cinder blocks. Cars had been hurled onto the parts of roof that remained intact. Walls had collapsed. Beams came crashing down. The parking lot stretched empty, devoid of cars, which the tornado had thrown into a nearby pond. And the weirdest detail of all: Horse manure from a nearby horse ranch clung to everything in stinking black clumps, Shelley remembers.

"It looked like a bomb went off outside," she says. "I had to warn the others about what they would see before they looked around."

And yet not a single student or staff member who huddled there in that nearly 700-member school passed away in the disaster. Not one.

For a school as large as Briarwood, it's jaw-droppingly astounding.

Shelley recalls watching in awe as the little first and second-graders, whose part of the school bore the brunt of the tornado's force, came climbing out of the rubble with the help of neighbors and friends. With their backpacks strapped on their backs as if headed home after a normal day. "We were very fortunate," says Shelley. "Only God could do something like that."

There were some injuries, of course, a few broken bones, but all of the kids, teachers, staff, and parents made it through the worst of the storm.

"They're so special and so brave," says Shelley. "After going through all that together we feel like a family, the kids, the teachers and staff."

Briarwood has been rebuilt, and Shelley says it's more beautiful than ever. The new school has far more modern technology than it used to, and everything's brand new and shiny.

"We still get cards and letters in the mail, even two years later, saying we're praying for you, we're thinking about you," says Shelley. "God was there. He was with everyone. Every teacher and staff member, plus there were parents who came to pick up kids. We had dads who protected kids with their own bodies. God was allowing everyone to do their jobs. Many of them still won't talk about what happened. They just quietly did what they were supposed to do."

Hero teachers. Dads. Moms. Recovery. God showing up. Giving peace. It's like we all got to experience a lifetime of hope, hurt, faith, and recovery all in just a few weeks time.

Tragedy made heroes out of ordinary people such as Dr. Shelley McMillan, Assistant Principal Jennifer Mankins, and the other teachers, staff, and parents.

This disaster impacted my view on pain and suffering, hope and overcoming. It was so widespread that the days following the tornado became a classroom for learning about problems and compassion.

For some people, the initial feelings would turn to relief. The tension would release. For others, it turned into an intense drive to help and serve, to do more and to inspire. For still others who experienced deeper loss, it would take months for homes to be rebuilt and possessions replaced.

But for those who lost the most, some are still walking in the darkness, unsure if morning will ever come. Some of these will learn to walk and live while still carrying the pain.

But will everyone recover? Will all overcome? No.

How is it that one person experiences devastating loss and it spurs them on to do great things and someone else experiences a similar devastating turn of events and they are chronically broken and even frozen in time throughout the rest of life? I wish I could answer that.

But even though we can't say for sure why some struggle more than others, we can gain comfort from God's word.

David, the shepherd-boy-turned-king is one of the most fascinating leaders in the Bible. As we discussed in chapter 3, he was a man who knew what walking through the darkest kinds of tragedy looked like.

Consider some of the tragedies David experienced. Besides the pain of his own broken family relationships, he was grieved by his mentor and father-figure King Saul. Though David loved him deeply, Saul's mental and spiritual breakdown resulted in the king spending his later years pursuing David to kill him. So David wasted months and years living in caves on the run. David's first born son died tragically as an infant, and later in life, his son Amnon raped his half sister Tamar, David's daughter. If that weren't tragic enough, Absalom, another of David's sons, killed Amnon in an act of vigilante justice. Then he tried to turn the hearts of the people against David, which forced a war.

Ultimately and tragically, for this passionate shepherd king and tender father, David had to then experience the death of his son Absalom, killed by David's own commanding officer. David knew tragedy.

A large part of the biblical book of Psalms was written by David, the poet, the musician, the sufferer. In some of these psalms, we find David's deepest heart cries.

Many scholars consider Psalm 139 to have been written by David late in his life. According to Dr. Timothy Eaton, Old Testament scholar, this particular Psalm may have been written so late in his life that some believe his son Solomon may have taken this writing and entered it into the collection.

Here's what David the experienced sufferer wrote late in life:

> You have searched me, Lord,
> and you know me.
> You know when I sit and when I rise;
> you perceive my thoughts from afar.
> You discern my going out and my lying down;
> you are familiar with all my ways.
> Before a word is on my tongue
> you, Lord, know it completely.
> You hem me in behind and before,
> and you lay your hand upon me.
> Such knowledge is too wonderful for me,
> too lofty for me to attain.
>
> Where can I go from your Spirit?
> Where can I flee from your presence?
> If I go up to the heavens, you are there;
> if I make my bed in the depths, you are there.
> If I rise on the wings of the dawn,
> if I settle on the far side of the sea,
> even there your hand will guide me,
> your right hand will hold me fast. (Psalm 139:1-10).

In other words, we're surrounded. Even if we tried to get away from God, it would be impossible. No matter where we go, or what we think, or what we do, He's one step ahead of us. "*Where can I go from your Spirit?*" David writes. "*Where can I flee from your presence?*" The understood response is nowhere. There is absolutely nowhere we can go where God is not intimately present. ***There is nothing that you could ever go through that our heavenly Father doesn't understand, and there is no dark place that He has not already walked.***

So when we ask the common question, "Where was God?" the answer from Scripture and from the experiences of many who have struggled is:

DURING LIFE'S STORMS, GOD IS ALWAYS NEAR.

Nathan and Amber Kriesel have three precious kids. When Nathan left for work on the morning of May 20, 2013, he had no idea about the horrors that would unfold that day. Amber stayed at home with their daughters, one six-year-old and four-year-old twins. By mid-afternoon, the tornado sirens blared all over the city, and Nathan rushed home just as the winds screamed and the tornado began to bear down.

When Nathan got into the house to join his family, the kids were already wearing bicycle helmets in the bathtub. Amber was there under a mattress. They prayed together. When the girls asked questions about what would happen, Nathan told his family this: that just like God was with Shadrach, Meshach and Abednego, three Hebrew children who were delivered by God from the furnace (Daniel 3), God would also be with them.

"Whatever happens," he said to them, "Jesus will save us."

These two parents stretched out over their kids. The walls began to shake. Nathan watched as the door disappeared first, and then the walls. Nathan and Amber were wedged between the tub and the toilet as the girls were in the bathtub, the tub lifted and started to twist. They prayed feverishly, knowing without God's strength that they would perish.

Just then, the winds calmed and settled. Nothing was left on the slab of their home besides this small section of tub and toilet. The mattress was gone. Nathan was battered and had debris even in his pockets and his ears. The girls didn't have a scratch.

The bathtub is now sitting in their back yard, and they've affectionately named it "The Ark." The girls are excited that they have their own story similar to the one in Genesis where God saved Noah and his family in the ark.

To this day, the Kreisels are the only family I've heard of that survived in open air against the 200-plus mile per hour winds of an EF5 tornado.

If you were to ask them, "Where was God, when your home was lost?" they would answer, "God is winning the hearts of our daughters."

"Even if we die today, Jesus will save us."

DURING LIFE'S STORMS, GOD IS ALWAYS NEAR.

Read again this poignant line from David's Psalm of lament and wisdom in Psalm 139:8:

"If I go up to the heavens, you are there; if I make my bed in the depths, you are there." Even in the darkest of valleys, the "depths."

Jackie and Amy Sing have known the Lord a long time. They have a committed walk with Jesus, and I've been honored to see them lead others to Him. Their home and everything they owned was destroyed on May 20, 2013. But they themselves were spared.

Right after the storm, national news trucks parked in the driveway in front of their ruined house and stayed there for nearly two weeks and repeatedly interviewed Jackie Sing, a quiet electrician from Moore. Day after day, God brought Scripture to his mind as he openly and unashamedly shared Christ with millions of viewers.

When I asked Jackie and Amy Sing, "Where was God when you lost all your precious memories, your home, your vehicles?"

Jackie's answer? "God was giving me, just a normal guy from Oklahoma, a platform to talk about Jesus openly and to help make Jesus famous."

DURING LIFE'S STORMS, GOD IS ALWAYS NEAR.

The psalmist David continues: *"If I rise on the wings of the dawn, if I settle on the far side of the sea, even there your hand will guide me, your right hand will hold me fast"* (Psalm 139:9-10).

Cyndi Beam, 42, a single woman who'd spent years in customer service, survived the Moore tragedy in her storm shelter. Cyndi was suffering from clinical depression, and she wasn't sure what the future held for her. She'd recently left her job of many years and was searching for purpose and meaning in her life when her computer radar showed a "big red splotch" south of Moore.

"Nobody ever expects it to be a 'big one,' and nobody ever expects it to happen to them," says Cyndi. So she wasn't in a hurry when hail began to hammer the roof of her house.

She hauled the last of her unwilling dogs down into the shelter, a concrete bunker with a vent on top, which she'd stocked with the usual survival supplies such as food, candles, and toilet paper, plus some oddities like an ax/crowbar combo just in case.

"I closed the hatch and twisted the handle," Cyndi remembers. "It was old and rusty so it took some doing, but I got it latched about a quarter of the way, then sat down on a lawn chair with a dog in my lap, wondering how long I would be in this hot little hole."

Within a few minutes she heard the roar of the tornado in the distance—a "train rumble"— and she found something to stick up into the vent to stop it from rotating.

"I started to hear a faint, high-pitched whistle, and it started getting louder," says Cyndi. "My hatch started rattling, so I grabbed the handle with both hands and pulled with all my might, letting my legs go limp and using my weight to pull it down. As it rattled up and down a bit, the bar turned inch by inch to the full 90-degree locked position. I stood frozen, still holding the handle like you do on a roller coaster ride, waiting for the storm to pass."

As the tornado bore down overhead, a recent Christian song by the band "Casting Crowns" suddenly popped into Cyndi's mind.

"During the approximately two minutes I was holding the door handle, I had 'Praise You In The Storm' running through my head," she recalls. "'The chorus came up: 'And I'll praise you in the storm, and I will lift my hands, for You are Who You are, no matter where I am.' I repeated the chorus to myself while holding my hands over my head, grasping the door handle for dear life. An overwhelming sense of peace washed over me. I thought, 'No matter what's happening outside of this shelter, God knows where I am. Whether my fence is missing or my house is missing, God knows where I am. Whether I live or die, God knows where I am."

"I had no fear," says Cyndi. "I was simply waiting for the storm to stop."

It was a life-changing moment for Cyndi.

"That sense of God's presence pressing into me was not only a comfort in that moment, as the tornado was ripping the neighborhood apart, but also as a reminder that He knows where I am in life," she says. "While I felt alone and unsure of my future, He knew what was coming next."

In fact, God had already given Cyndi uncanny foresight when she purchased the ax/crowbar combo, figuring it was a waste of $35. But because the latch on the hatch had stuck shut, she had to pound it open with her crowbar, something she'd never really anticipated having to use. When she lifted the hatch about four inches, she should have seen the privacy fence to the south. Instead, all she saw was dark gray sky with wreckage underneath. Her neighbor's house was in shambles.

"Except for about eight feet of chimney, I was taller than my house," she says. "It had been reduced to nothing but bricks, sticks, and 'buried treasure' under the rubble. My car was totaled. Many people have used the word 'surreal' to describe the scene that day, but that word doesn't even come close."

Yet Cyndi never lost her sense of humor.

"My house is gone," she texted a friend. "I hope it landed on a wicked witch somewhere."

After that day, Cyndi was never the same. Emboldened by what God had done and what she'd survived, she used her natural wit and overcoming spirit and began sharing her testimony with groups, and talking to survivors and volunteers as they worked on restoring the homes and hearts of Moore residents. She wrote articles and blogs about the experiences, and after that she took a position with the church, helping others who'd lost everything to find disaster relief support.

When I asked Cyndi Beam, "Where was God when everything you owned would fit into the backseat of your destroyed car?" she said with great confidence, "When I was in the shelter, something happened within me. God was giving me new hope, new purpose, and a new future."

DURING LIFE'S STORMS, GOD IS ALWAYS NEAR.

"If I say, 'Surely the darkness will hide me and the light become night around me…'" (Psalm 139:11).

Chase and Alise Newby, ages 36 and 30, are good friends of mine and active at our church. Chase left for work on the morning of May 20th to go to his IT job. Because of some technical difficulties at the office, he initially didn't realize that the storm was coming. Alise was at home with their youngest son, Noah, age 3, plus their two dogs and cat.

As the tornado sirens went off, Alise hurried into a storm shelter a few doors down from their home, which stood right across the street from Plaza Towers Elementary School. By the time Alise and Noah had closed themselves in the shelter, she regretted not going to get her oldest son, Liam, age 6, out of school.

The shelter shook. The tornado screamed outside, air pressure changes squeezed and popped their eardrums, making it almost unbearable. Neighbors huddling in the shelter cried and prayed as they waited for the storm to pass. All Alise could think about was Liam.

As soon as Alise stepped out of the shelter, she saw a pile of debris where the school had previously stood. A large cinder block wall had collapsed right where Liam's first grade class should have been.

After a few panic-filled moments, she found that her precious son, Liam was fine with barely a scratch. But how did he survive? Much later in the day they discovered the truth: the teachers, young women with families, empty nesters looking forward to retirement, from every age and life stage – these teachers had all heroically sacrificed themselves and laid their own bodies across the kids in the hallways.

In the case of young Liam Newby and two of his other classmates, their teacher and hero, Karen Marinelli, had thrown herself over their tiny bodies to protect them. When a car smashed through the cinder block wall and the wall crushed her back and pelvis, she offered her own life to save her three precious first graders.

Karen lived, and she was lifted from the rubble and hailed a hero.

If you ask Alise Newby, "Where was God when you lost your home, when you couldn't find your son?" Her reply? "God gave us a precious gift when He gave us our son. Now He gave us another miracle when He gave us Karen Marinelli."

If you ask Chase Newby, "Where was God?" His response? "I've seen so much evidence of God through this storm. I've seen so many things that point directly to Him, like God was coming beside me and helping me to find my own faith."

Chase and Alise, you see, were baptized together the very next year on Easter Sunday.

If you ask Karen Marinelli, "Where was God when the school was crashing in?" What does she say? "He was giving us strength to protect the kids, and using us to help them even though we were completely terrified."

DURING LIFE'S STORMS, GOD IS ALWAYS NEAR.

David continues reflecting on what God is like even when things are dark...

"...even the darkness will not be dark to you; the night will shine like the day, for darkness is as light to you" (Psalm 139:12).

Remember Scott and Stacey's precious boy, Nicolas McCabe? The wiry third-grade boy went to Plaza Towers Elementary School. He was vibrant, energetic, loving, and generous with a funny quirk. Every day he would ask his parents for "extras"—extra money. Extra snacks. Extra pepperonis in his lunch. Scott and Stacey had no idea why their rambunctious eight-year-old always asked for extras.

On the morning of May 20, teachers at Plaza Towers Elementary School held an assembly for the end of the school year. The word of the day was *"courage."* Later that day, instead of going home to be with Scott and Stacey, "Nic-Nic" went home to be with Jesus.

A few days after the tragedy, a counselor told the McCabes what Nicolas did with his extras. Every day, he would take his extra money and buy things for other kids, such as snacks or a drink. He would share what was in his own lunch. His pepperonis. His chips. Half his sandwich. The McCabes had no idea.

Ask Stacey McCabe, "Where was God when young Nicolas passed away?" She confidently answers, "He was right there. Where He's always been. Because of this, his daddy was able to come to know Jesus. If that was the purpose of my son's death, then it was worth it."

The rest of us also, myself included, have learned from young Nicolas, about life, love, and especially unsung and anonymous generosity.

DURING LIFE'S STORMS, GOD IS ALWAYS NEAR.

Many people try to answer the question "Why?" when bad things happen. When the storms of life roll in. When tragedy strikes.

Philosophers and theologians have tried to answer this question academically in so many different ways. Here are a few examples of mankind's attempts to answer the question of suffering:

- » Suffering makes us like Christ.
- » God plans to glorify Himself by raising us up after tragedy.
- » There's a bigger picture that we can't understand.
- » God is trying to get our attention.
- » It's to show ourselves how much we trust God.
- » It's to show us what is wrong with the world so we long for something better.

There are so many other possible explanations that we couldn't even cover them all in a book of this size. Maybe there's a degree of truth in all of these ideas. But when we're going through a hard time, not a single academic concept or answer gives us comfort.

WE CANNOT EVER FULLY ANSWER THE QUESTION "WHY?"

To answer such a question, we'd have to literally know the mind of God. In fact, this question of pain and suffering that we've tackled in this book is probably the most difficult question for us to face.

I agree with Dr. John Lennox of Oxford. My paraphrase of a statement Dr. Lennox makes frequently is this, since we can't for certain know the reason for our pain, we have to ask the next question:

IS GOD TRUSTWORTHY? CAN I TRUST HIM EVEN WITH THE PAIN?

Yes. I've found the answer to be a resounding and clear "Yes." Countless others have found Him right at the darkest place in the darkest hour and in the darkest experience of life.

That's why instead of attempting to answer the question "why?" we've asked a different question in this book. The question we want to reflect on is, "Where is God when I'm struggling?"

Here is some evidence of God's presence that we've discovered through the struggles discussed in this book.

» God was there bringing thousands of compassionate cops, firefighters, medics, and first responders like Rhett Burnett who rushed to the disaster when the rest of us were rushing away.

» God was with the heroic teachers of Briarwood, Plaza Towers, and Highland East Jr. High as they protected students, sacrificed, and lead well through this tragedy.

» God was inspiring principals like Amy Simpson and Dr. Shelley McMillan who led with grace, poise, and confidence through something they were never specifically trained for.

» God was sending tens of thousands of spiritual leaders like Sam Porter and Bunny Yekzamen to help rescue, recover, then offer help with relief and rebuilding.

» God was helping Jason Head to understand the fatherhood of God even though his own father was abusive.

» God was providing for single mother Hilarey Phillips during her leukemia diagnosis.

- » God was elevating LaTara Bussey's influence as she overcame her abuse and hurt.
- » God was bringing my family closer together and closer to Himself during Chrysty's illness.
- » God was bringing Scott McCabe to the point of knowing Jesus through Nicolas' death.
- » God was restoring James and Micah Moody's faith in humanity as people from all over came to support them when they lost their home.
- » God was calling Kari and Kayla Carmona to minister in Moore and receive more healing themselves in the process.
- » God was strengthening the Newby's marriage and faith.

God was involved in literally tens of thousands of other ways. It's not hard to see the evidence of God's presence during our struggles.

It's important to understand that God's ultimate purpose for us is for us to become like Christ. Every single thing that we ever go through is a tool that can be used to drive us towards that purpose.

Author Tim Keller summarized Martin Luther's statement of suffering beautifully in this way: "Suffering is unbearable if you aren't certain that God is for you and with you."[40]

---

40 Cited in *Walking With God through Pain and Suffering*, Timothy Keller (New York: Penguin Group, 2013), 58.

In the middle of pain, many ***run*** from God.

In the middle of pain, many others ***find*** God.

If you're in the dark stormy night of family problems, abuse, or loneliness, God is there.

If your relationships that were once peaceful are falling apart, God is there.

If your life seems to be one long series of hardships and injustices after another, God is there.

If your house feels empty without your kids, if your womb feels empty without your child, if your life feels empty without a husband or wife, even when you feel you have no purpose at all, God is there.

If you're wondering if you can ever find Him or if He cares about you at all, He's there.

Cry out to God! Ask Him to show Himself to you. Ask Him to bring His peace into your troubled sea and to calm your storm.

Jesus says, "Ask and it will be given to you; seek and you will find; knock and the door will be opened to you. For everyone who asks receives; the one who seeks finds; and to the one who knocks, the door will be opened" (Matthew 7:7-8).

Maybe the great secret to finding God in life's storms isn't a secret after all.

Maybe in order to find God in life's storms, I need only to seek Him out.

I pray that you seek Him as you find yourself in the midst of life's storms.

In the best of circumstances and in the worst of situations, God is always right there beside us.

DURING LIFE'S STORMS, GOD IS ALWAYS NEAR.

To hear more of Cyndi Beam's story and even more stories of hope and Use the QR code below or go to www.WhereWasGod.com/book.

ABOUT THE AUTHORS

When they were only 17 and far too young by most standards, Steven Earp married Chrysty, his sweetheart since junior high. In spite of their early wedding, they've now had 20 great years of marriage (and a couple of rough ones!) They have five great kids: Alyssa (22) who just married Tyler; Kimmy (20) who is about to marry Wesley; John-Mark (16), Mikayla (15) and Jeremy (13), all still at home.

Steven planted and pastors Elevate Church in Moore, Oklahoma, the community where he has spent most of his life. Before pastoring Elevate, the Earps spent most of their adult lives serving churches and simultaneously operating businesses to fund ministry.

He works extensively with recruiting, training, coaching, and resourcing church planters. As far as hobbies go, he likes to think he's a nerd. But actually, he's not committed enough to any one particular brand of nerdhood to qualify. Perhaps he's more of a "shade-tree" nerd.

You can find out more about Steven and his writing at
StevenEarp.com

Jennifer Rogers Spinola is a writer, speaker, and author of four Christian fiction novels, including 2011 Christy Awards finalist *Southern Fried Sushi*. She previously served as a short-term missionary in Japan through the Southern Baptist International Mission Board, where she met her Brazilian husband, Athos. Jennifer spent more than eight years in Brazil as a wife and mom, and she's passionate about adoption, missions, Japanese art, Brazilian coffee, and all things redneck.

When she's not writing, Jennifer is changing diapers, homeschooling her wild and wonderful boys, and hunting for mismatched socks.

CPSIA information can be obtained
at www.ICGtesting.com
Printed in the USA
FSOW03n0748311215
15040FS